Fair Isle
FASHION KNITS

Fair Isle FASHION KNITS

17 Top-Down Designs in Allover Stranded Colorwork Patterns

ANDREA BRAUNEIS

STACKPOLE BOOKS

Essex, Connecticut
Blue Ridge Summit, Pennsylvania

STACKPOLE BOOKS

An imprint of The Globe Pequot Publishing Group, Inc.
64 South Main Street
Essex, CT 06426
www.globepequot.com

Distributed by NATIONAL BOOK NETWORK

© Edition Michael Fischer GmbH, 2023
www.emf-verlag.de
This edition of *Nordische Pullover Stricken* first published in Germany by Edition Michael Fischer GmbH in 2023 is published by arrangement with Silke Bruenink Agency, Munich, Germany.

Book layout and typesetting: Theresa Bull
Product management: Melanie Kowalski
Images: © Corinna Teresa Brix, Munich, Germany; Illustrations in chapter Basics:
© Ina Langguth, Berlin, Germany; Images and text for Italian bind-off in chapter Basics:
© Andrea Brauneis
Translation: Katharina Sokiran

We have made every effort to ensure the accuracy and completeness of these instructions. We cannot, however, be responsible for human error, typographical mistakes, or variations in individual work.

British Library Cataloguing in Publication Information available

Library of Congress Cataloging-in-Publication Data

Names: Brauneis, Andrea, author. | Sokiran, Katharina, translator.
Title: Fair Isle fashion knits : 17 top-down designs in allover stranded colorwork patterns /
  Andrea Brauneis ; translation Katharina Sokiran.
Other titles: Nordische pullover striken. English
Description: Essex, Connecticut ; Blue Ridge Summit, Pennsylvania : Stackpole Books, [2025] |
  Text in English. Translation from German.
Identifiers: LCCN 2024026907 (print) | LCCN 2024026908 (ebook) | ISBN 9780811774895
  (paperback) | ISBN 9780811774901 (ebook)
Subjects: LCSH: Knitting—Patterns.
Classification: LCC TT825 .B693 2025 (print) | LCC TT825 (ebook) | DDC 746.43/2041—dc23/
  eng/20240703
LC record available at https://lccn.loc.gov/2024026907
LC ebook record available at https://lccn.loc.gov/2024026908

CONTENTS

PREFACE

It all began on a small island called Fair Isle . . .

. . . and today, every knitting enthusiast, no matter in what corner of the world, knows that this is the high art of knitting, where true works of art are created using two or more colors in a row or round.

This book is for all knitters who, like me, love this technique, but sometimes also want to diverge from traditional styles and stitch patterns.

In this book, you will find 17 designs from simple to somewhat more sophisticated. The patterns are not intended for beginning knitters, as prior knowledge of required knitting techniques is assumed. Nevertheless, knitters new to Fair Isle can very well discover the joy of this great art here.

All patterns are worked from the top down using different techniques. I've carefully selected easy stitch patterns with short floats so that knitting through to the end of the chosen project will always be pleasant and the result simply stunning.

With that, I have almost given away too much already! You certainly want to browse through the book on your own to discover the patterns and techniques and choose your favorite designs.

Enjoy the process of choosing and knitting your favorites, and wear the results with as much pride as I do!

Yours sincerely,

Andrea Brauneis

Basics

STRANDED COLORWORK

Summarizing the history of stranded colorwork as well as the countless possibilities offered by this great technique cannot possibly be accomplished in just a few words, which would not do justice to the history, the evolution, and the finer points of the technique. However, I would like to give you at least a short summary:

The Fair Isle stranded colorwork technique has its origin on the island of the same name, Fair Isle, a Scottish island belonging to the Shetland Islands. Located between Orkney and Shetland and consisting of scarcely 8 square kilometers, this smallest island of the group is populated by just 55 permanent residents. Legend says that around 1588, a Spanish ship was shipwrecked off the island, and the sailors who took refuge on the island, as a thank you, showed the islanders how to knit with many colorful yarns at the same time.

On this cold and poor island, knitting in this technique, which quickly became characteristic of the island, soon became the only way of earning a living for many families who supported themselves by selling knitwear on the mainland. To this day, local women knit in this technique, creating true works of art.

In the meantime, this type of knitting also became popular in other countries, where each developed its own typical patterns. You can often tell from which country a knitted piece comes by the motifs (a perfect example being the traditional Norwegian star).

TECHNIQUES

HOLDING THE WORKING YARN

Traditionally, Scandinavian colorwork patterns are worked with 2 colors in each row or round, though sometimes with more than 2 colors in a row or round. For this book, I've chosen only colorwork patterns with no more than 2 colors per row or round.

There are different methods of holding the working yarn. I show the easiest one here, once with using a yarn guide, once without it. Regardless of how you hold the working yarn or which knitting technique you use, once established, the position of the strands should not be changed during knitting to ensure an even stitch appearance. It is best to try out in a small swatch which method suits you best.

In stranded colorwork knitting, one yarn always appears dominant; this is referred to as yarn dominance. The dominant yarn is the yarn that has to cover a longer distance to the next stitch; therefore, this is the strand in the motif color carried in the back, which is usually held to the left of the main/background color. Here, too, it is not that important which specific way you hold the working yarns in your hand, as long as the motif color is always held at the left so it will arrange itself under or over the main/background color on the wrong side of the fabric, and the yarns are held at an even tension.

Lead both strands to the back over the left index finger, always holding the motif color to the left of the main/background color. Pick up the working yarn in the current color to be worked with the right needle, knit the st, and let it slip off the needle. Holding your fingertips close to the needles will allow you to better control tension.

Holding the yarns using a yarn guide or knitting thimble

Thread the motif color through the left yarn guide of the ring, and the main/background color through the right one. Every knitter has their own preference for holding the yarn guide—the picture shows how I hold mine. Work the sts as previously described.

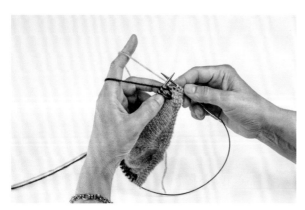

Holding the yarns over the left index finger

FLOATS

In stranded colorwork, the motif color is carried on the wrong side of the fabric in the form of a "float." To ensure that the right side of the fabric shows even and smooth stitches, the contrasting-color floats in the back of the work should always be located below, with the main/background yarn above them. A float should never span more than 4 stitches; longer floats are prone to becoming taut and pulling the fabric in. While knitting, push the stitches on the right needle apart—this way, the carried yarn will cover the same distance as the newly formed stitches.

Float

Change from motif color to main/background color

Pull the working yarn in the motif color through under the strand in the main color and knit the required number of sts.

Carrying the unused working yarn in back of work

In back of the work, the floats always need to be parallel and should not be twisted around each other. To ensure an even stitch appearance, the working yarn in one color always needs to run consistently either over or under the strand in the other color.

Locking in the strands

This is recommended in pattern sections where you would carry a yarn over more than 4 stitches (to avoid long floats), as well as for joining new working yarn. Work to the spot where the float should be caught and cross the strands in back of the work. To do this, work with both strands over at least 6–8 stitches widthwise, locking in the unused color or yarn by alternatingly knitting the active strand under and over the strand to be locked in, then working the stitch. Excess ends can be trimmed afterwards. This eliminates the need for weaving in the remaining ends later.

INCREASES

INCREASING 1 STITCH (INC 1)

Right-leaning lifted increase

Work to the stitch *before* which the increase is supposed to be worked. Now, insert the right needle from back to front into the right leg of the stitch below the next stitch, lift it onto the left needle, and knit it.

Left-leaning lifted increase

Work to the stitch *after* which the increase is supposed to be worked. Now, insert the left needle from back to front into the left leg of the stitch below the stitch just worked (on the right needle), lift it onto the left needle, and knit it.

PLEASE NOTE

Some yarns tend to produce a small hole in the increase spot. If this happens, knit the stitch through the back loop (twisted).

INCREASE FROM THE BAR BETWEEN STITCHES (M1 FROM THE BAR BETWEEN STITCHES)

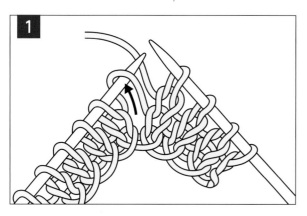

Using the left needle, pick up the bar before the next stitch from front to back.

(Not shown: Alternatively, you can pick up the bar before the next stitch from back to front with the right needle, depending on which method you like better.)

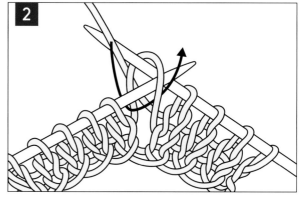

Depending on the specific instructions given in each pattern, either knit or purl the bar between stitches through the back loop (twisted).

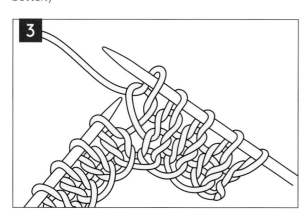

This is how the completed stitch looks.

DECREASES

KNITTING 2 STITCHES TOGETHER RIGHT-LEANING (K2TOG)

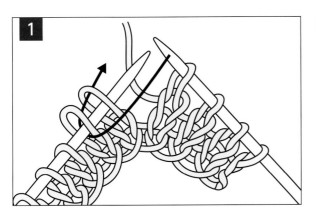

Insert the right needle from left to right first into the stitch after the next one, then into the next stitch on the left needle.

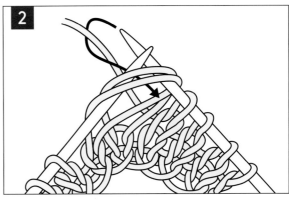

Knit both stitches together.

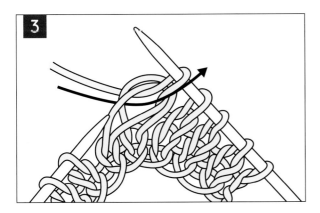

Let both stitches slip off the left needle. Both are now leaning to the right.

KNITTING 2 STITCHES TOGETHER LEFT-LEANING WITH PASSING OVER

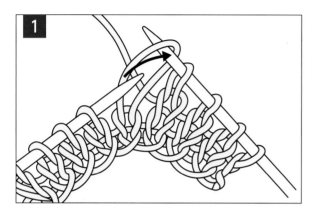

Slip the 1st stitch on the left needle knitwise.

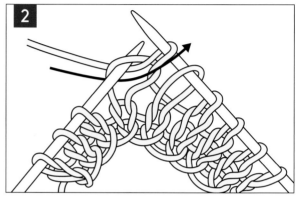

Knit the next stitch.

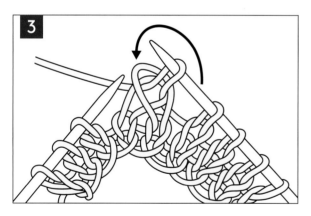

Now, pass the slipped stitch over the knitted one.

KNITTING 3 STITCHES TOGETHER LEFT-LEANING WITH PASSING OVER (SL1-K2TOG-PSSO)

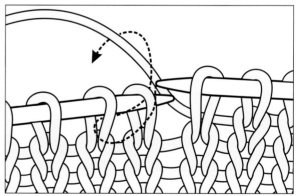

Slip the 1st stitch on the left needle knitwise. Now, knit the next 2 stitches together, and pass the slipped stitch over the stitches knitted together.

GERMAN SHORT ROWS

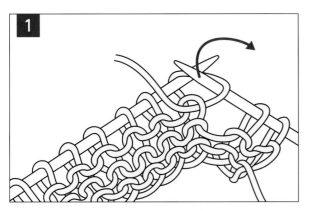

Work as many stitches as stated in the instructions, turn work, move the working yarn to the front of the work, and slip the next stitch purlwise.

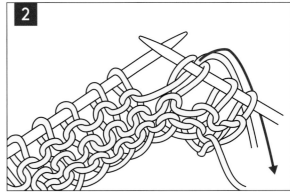

Now, pull the working yarn to the back over the needle until it produces a double stitch with two legs sitting on the needle. It can be helpful to put a stitch marker through both legs to help identify them later.

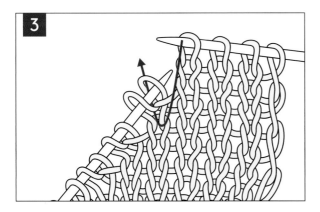

To work the double stitch later, insert the right needle through both visible legs, and either knit or purl both legs together as one, depending on the pattern.

ITALIAN BIND-OFF

The Italian bind-off creates an elastic and neat-looking bound-off edge, using a dull tapestry needle.

Break the working yarn leaving a tail at least three times as long as the planned width of the row of stitches to bind off. Insert the tapestry needle from right to left through the selvedge stitch and the following stitch.

Let both stitches slip off the knitting needle, and firmly tighten the working yarn.

From here on, stitches are always bound off in pairs: Insert the needle from left to right into the 1st (purl) stitch on the left needle and pull the yarn taut; leave this stitch on the knitting needle.

Now, insert the tapestry needle from right to left through the middle of the preceding knit stitch (which is no longer on the knitting needle), then pull it through the 2nd (knit) stitch on the left needle, and pull the yarn taut, leaving the stitches on the needle.

Now, insert the tapestry needle from right to left into the 1st stitch still sitting on the needle. Tighten the yarn firmly and let the pair of stitches slip off the knitting needle. Then, repeat Steps 3–5 until all stitches have been bound off.

BINDING OFF WITH APPLIED I-CORD

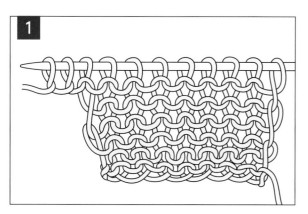

Using the backwards loop cast-on method, cast on as many new stitches as stated in the pattern—for the pictured sample this is 2 stitches. This is easier to accomplish at the end of the previous row; then turn work.

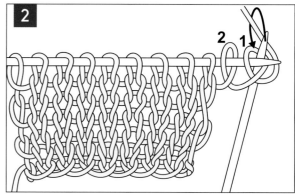

Knit the newly cast-on stitches.

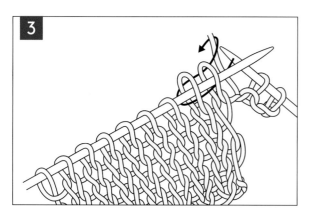

Knit the next stitch on the left needle together with the following stitch through the back loop left-leaning.

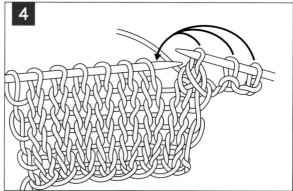

Place the 3 stitches from the right needle one by one back onto the left needle, then repeat the working steps shown in illustrations 2 through 4 to the last 3 stitches. Knit these 3 stitches together, break the working yarn, and pull it through the last stitch to secure.

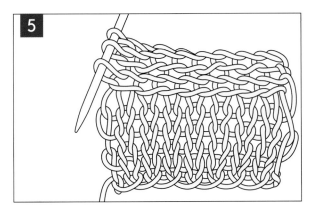

The finished I-cord edge looks like a cord placed horizontally.

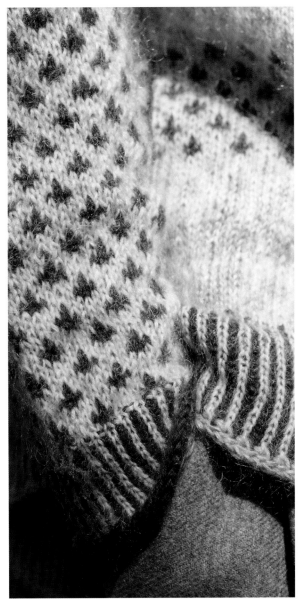

MATTRESS STITCH

Side seams can be joined neatly using the mattress stitch. By gently tightening the working yarn from time to time, the selvedge stitches will be pulled to the wrong side of the fabric, where they are hidden in the seam. This creates an almost invisible seam.

Mattress stitch for stockinette

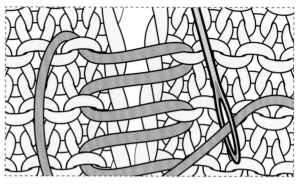

Mattress stitch for garter stitch

Place the edges of the pieces to be joined next to each other, right sides facing up, and, using a tapestry needle, on the piece located at the left, pick up the bars between the 2 stitches located between the selvedge stitches and the respective 1st knit stitch. Then, insert the tapestry needle from bottom to top below the two bars between the two corresponding stitches on the opposite piece. Repeat these steps to the end of the edges, regularly tightening the working yarn gently as you proceed.

For garter stitch fabric, insert the needle from bottom to top alternatingly into the right and the left piece. While doing this, at the left edge, always take up the upward-pointing bumps of the stitch; at the right edge, on the other hand, the downward-pointing bumps of the stitch.

MATTRESS STITCH FOR OTHER STITCH PATTERNS

The mattress stitch can be worked in a similar way for all other stitch patterns. Since it is worked on the right side of the knitted fabric, it is always clearly visible how the seam fits into the stitch pattern.

READING KNITTING CHARTS AND DECIPHERING ABBREVIATIONS

In every knitting chart, the stitch pattern is shown in a symbolic way, with every box of the chart representing one action to be performed. Right-side rows in the chart are read from right to left in the direction of the actual knitting, wrong-side rows from left to right, always from bottom to top.

ABBREVIATIONS

approx.	=	approximately
BOR	=	beginning of the round
inc	=	increase
k1b	=	knit 1 below
k2tog	=	knit 2 sts together right-leaning
kfb	=	knit the same st through the front and back (1 st increased)
m	=	stitch marker
M1L	=	inc 1 st left-leaning knitwise from the bar between sts (1 st increased)
M1R	=	inc 1 st right-leaning knitwise from the bar between sts (1 st increased)
pfb	=	purl the same st through the front and back (1 st increased)
rep	=	repeat
Rg-st(s)	=	raglan stitch(es)
RS	=	right-side (row)
selv st(s)	=	selvedge stitch(es)
skp	=	slip, knit, pass (1 st decreased)
sl	=	slip the st without working it
sl1-k2tog-psso	=	slip 1, knit the next 2 sts together, pass the slipped st over (2 sts decreased)
sl2-k2tog-psso	=	slip 2, knit the next 2 sts together, pass the slipped sts over (3 sts decreased)
ssk	=	slip, slip, knit slipped sts together (1 st decreased)
ssp	=	slip, slip, purl slipped sts together (1 st decreased)
sssk	=	slip, slip, slip, knit slipped sts together (2 sts decreased)
st(s)	=	stitch(es)
tbl	=	through the back loop
WS	=	wrong-side (row)
yo	=	yarn over

DIFFICULTY LEVELS

◆◇◇	=	easy
◆◆◇	=	intermediate
◆◆◆	=	advanced

Projects

ROYA
Short-sleeved raglan sweater

◆◆◆

SIZES

S (M/L/XL)

Chest Circumference

36.5 (39.5/43.25/47.25) in/93 (100/110/120) cm

Total Length

22.5 in/57 cm

MATERIALS

- Lang Yarns Mohair Luxe; DK weight; 77% mohair, 23% silk; 191.5 yd/175 m per 0.9 oz/25 g

  Black 0004: 3 (3/4/4) skeins

  Light Blue 0133: 3 (3/4/4) skeins

- Lang Yarns Merino 400 Lace; sock/baby weight; 100% extra fine merino wool; 219 yd/200 m per 0.9 oz/25 g

  Black 0004: 3 (3/4/4) skeins

  Light Blue 0034: 3 (3/4/4) skeins

- US size 6 (4 mm) and 7 (4.5 mm) circular knitting needles in different lengths

- US size 7 (4.5 mm) double-pointed needle set for sleeve ribbing, if desired

- Stitch markers

- Stitch holder, extra needles or cords, or waste yarn for holding stitches

- Tapestry needle

- Scissors

GAUGE

In pattern on US 7 (4.5 mm) needles: 24 sts and 26 rows = 4 x 4 in (10 x 10 cm)

STITCH PATTERNS

Main Pattern

Stockinette stitch in charted colorwork pattern in the indicated order of work.

Raglan Stitches

2 sts in stockinette stitch in Light Blue.

Increases

Please refer to illustrated tutorials in Basics chapter on page 17–18

INSTRUCTIONS

Roya is worked from the top down with raglan increases.

Work with 1 strand of Mohair Luxe in Black held together with 1 strand of Merino 400 Lace in Black, and 1 strand of Mohair Luxe in Light Blue held together with 1 strand of Merino 400 Lace in Light Blue.

TIP

Before starting work, wind the 2 strands of the same color together into 1 skein

NECK BAND

Using US 6 (4.0 mm) needles and Light Blue, cast on 128 (128/136/136) sts, then join into the round, taking care not to twist the cast-on row. Place a marker to indicate the BOR.

Work 2 rounds in Light Blue in stockinette stitch.

Work 5 rounds of ribbing as follows: *K2 in Light Blue, p2 in Black*, rep from * to *.

RAGLAN

Change to US 7 (4.5 mm) needles, and work the pattern repeat according to the chart.

Raglan increases are worked in every other round as follows:

Rnd 1 (Rnd 1 of the chart in Light Blue): Place m, k2 (Rg-sts), place m, **inc 1**, k18 (right sleeve), **inc 1**, place m, k2 (Rg-sts), place m, **inc 1**, k42 (42/46/46) front sts, **inc 1**, place m, k2 (Rg-sts), place m, **inc 1**, k18 (left sleeve), **inc 1**, place m, k2 (Rg-sts), **inc 1**, k42 (42/46/46) back sts, **inc 1**. (8 sts increased) [= 136 (136/144/144) sts].

Slip all markers as you encounter them.

Rnd 2 (Rnd 2 of the chart in Light Blue): Work 2 sts (Rg-sts), work 20 sts (right sleeve), work 2 sts (Rg-sts), work 44 (44/48/48) sts (front), work 2 sts (Rg-sts), work 20 sts (left sleeve), work 2 sts (Rg-sts), work 44 (44/48/48) sts (back).

Rnds 3 and 4: Work as Rnds 1 and 2.

Divide the sts in sections as follows, using markers: 22 sts for each sleeve, 46 (46/50/50) sts each for Front/Back (+8 Rg-sts) [= 144 (144/152/152) sts].

Rnd 5 (Rnd 5 of the chart): 2 Rg-sts in Light Blue, **inc 1 in Black**, *2 sts in Light Blue, 2 sts in Black*, work from * to * 5 times total, 2 sts in Light Blue, **inc 1 in Black**, 2 Rg-sts in Light Blue, **inc 1 in Black**, *2 sts in Light Blue, 2 sts in Black*, work from * to * 11 (11/12/12) times total, 2 sts in Light Blue, **inc 1 in Black**, 2 Rg-sts in Light Blue, **inc 1 in Black**, *2 sts in Light Blue, 2 sts in Black*, work from * to * 5 times total, 2 sts in Light Blue, **inc 1 in Black**, 2 Rg-sts in Light Blue, **inc 1 in Black**, *2 sts in Light Blue, 2 sts in Black*, work from * to * 11 (11/12/12) times total, 2 sts in Light Blue, **inc 1 in Black** (8 sts increased) [= 152 (152/160/160) sts].

Rnd 6 (Rnd 6 of the chart): Slip the BOR marker. 2 Rg-sts in Light Blue, 1 st in Black, *2 sts in Light Blue, 2 sts in Black*, work from * to * 5 times total, 2 sts in Light Blue, 1 st in Black, 2 Rg-sts in Light Blue, 1 st in Black, *2 sts in Light Blue, 2 sts in Black*, work from * to * 11 (11/12/12) times total, 2 sts in Light Blue, 1 st in Black, 2 Rg-sts in Light Blue, 1 st in Black, *2 sts in Light Blue, 2 sts in Black*, work from * to * 5 times total, 2 sts in Light Blue, 1 st in Black, 2 Rg-sts in Light Blue, 1 st in Black, *2 sts in Light Blue, 2 sts in Black*, work from * to * 11 (11/12/12) times total, 2 sts in Light Blue, 1 st in Black.

Now, continue according to the chart, and rep Raglan increases 27 (31/33/37) times more.

Divide the sts in sections as follows, using markers: 78 (86/90/98) sts for each sleeve, 102 (110/118/126) sts each for front and back (+ 8 Rg-sts) [= 368 (400/424/456) sts].

DIVIDING THE SLEEVES FROM THE BODY

Remove all markers.

Work 2 sts (Rg-sts), transfer 78 (86/90/98) sts (right sleeve) to a stitch holder or piece of waste yarn for holding, cast on 6 (6/10/14) new underarm sts with both strands of working yarn held together, placing a new marker in the middle after 3 (3/5/7) sts (= BOR), incorporate 2 Rg-sts into the stitch pattern, work 102 (110/118/126) sts (front) in pattern, incorporate 2 Rg-sts into the stitch pattern, transfer 78 (86/90/98) sts (left sleeve) to a stitch holder or piece of waste yarn for holding, cast on 6 (6/10/14) new underarm sts with both strands of working yarn held together, incorporate 2 Rg-sts into the stitch pattern, work 102 (110/118/126) sts (back) in pattern, incorporate 2 Rg-sts into the stitch pattern, incorporate the newly cast-on underarm sts into the stitch pattern [= 224 (240/264/288) sts].

Continue, working from the chart, until the pattern rep has been worked 5 times heightwise (140 rounds), approx. 22.5 in/57 cm from cast-on. Bind off all sts knitwise in Light Blue.

SLEEVES

Take up the formerly held 78 (86/90/98) sleeve sts with a short circular knitting needle or a double-pointed needle set.

In Black, pick up and knit 6 (6/10/14) sts from the newly cast-on underarm sts (placing a new marker in the middle of the sts to indicate the BOR), and join into the round [= 84 (92/100/112) sts].

Work 1 round in Black in stockinette stitch.

In the next round, decrease 12 (14/16/18) sts evenly spaced [= 72 (78/84/94) sts].

In Black, work 4 rounds in ribbing pattern: *K1, p1*, rep from * to *.

Bind off all sts in pattern.

FINISHING

Carefully weave in all ends. Spread the sweater out flat on an even surface, pull it into shape, cover it with wet cloths, and let it dry.

CHART

The chart is worked 5 times heightwise as stated in the pattern instructions.

GLENNA
Hooded cardigan

◆◆◆

SIZES

S (M/L/XL/XXL)

Chest Circumference

35.5 (39.5/43.25/47.25/51.25) in/90 (100/110/120/130) cm

Length from Underarm

15.8 in/40 cm

Total Length

20.5 (21.25/22/22.75/23.5) in/52 (54/56/58/60) cm

MATERIALS

- Isager Aran Tweed; medium/worsted weight; 100% wool; 175 yd/160 m per 3.5 oz/100 g

  Rosé: 4 (4/5/5/5) skeins

  Sand: 4 (4/5/5/5) skeins

- Five 1 in/26 mm buttons (buttons shown in sample are Agoya mother-of-pearl buttons by Jim Knopf in Pink)

- US size 9 (5.5 mm) circular knitting needles in different lengths

- US size 9 (5.5 mm) double-pointed needle set for the sleeves, if desired

- Stitch markers

- Tapestry needle

- Scissors

GAUGE

In pattern: 16 sts and 24 rows = 4 x 4 in (10 x 10 cm)

STITCH PATTERNS

Main Pattern

Stockinette stitch in charted colorwork pattern in the indicated order of work.

Pattern with Knit Stitches Worked in Rows Below

Knit 1 below (k1b): Insert the right needle into the st located directly below the next st on the left needle, pull the working yarn through, and let the old st drop from the left needle. The st above dissolves (now looking like a st with a yarn over).

RS: *K1b, p1*, rep from * to * continuously.

WS: *P1, k1*, rep from * to * continuously.

Selvedge Stitches

Please refer to the specific instructions listed in this pattern.

Short Rows

Please refer to illustrated tutorial in Basics chapter on page 21.

CONSTRUCTION NOTES

The cardigan is worked from the top down.

First, the hood is worked. The back and the shoulders are formed from the stitches in the center back of the hood. The fronts are knitted directly onto the shoulders, also incorporating the stitches at the sides of the hood, creating a seamless transition. Then, the sleeves are knitted directly onto the selv sts of the front and shoulders. Here, multiple steps are worked at the same time, therefore, it is important to read through the instructions carefully and annotate them if necessary.

INSTRUCTIONS

HOOD

The hood is worked in Rosé throughout.

Using a circular knitting needle with long cord, cast on 21 sts, then work a setup row on the WS as follows:

P1 (selv st), *p1, k1*, rep from * to * 8 times more, p1, p1 (selv st).

Row 1 (RS): K1 (selv st), *k1b, p1*, rep from * to * 8 times more, k1b, knit the selv st.

Row 2 (WS): P1 (selv st), *p1, k1*, rep from * to * 8 times more, p1, purl the selv st.

Work Rows 1 and 2 a total of 24 times (48 rows).

Leave the live sts on the needle, break the working yarn.

Now, sts will be picked up and knit from the edges of the knitted piece. From the right edge of the knitted piece, pick up and knit 26 sts, beginning at the cast-on row.

TIP

At this point, you must knit around the corner. It will be easier to work similarly to the Magic Loop method (i.e., pulling out the cord between the sts so that it will be convenient to work along the side of the knitted piece).

Pull the cord of the circular needle out between the sts and into a loop and work the live 21 sts continuing in pattern, then pull the cord of the circular needle into another loop, and pick up and knit 26 sts from the left edge of the knitted piece, ending at the cast-on row [= 73 sts].

Turn work and work a WS row as follows:

Purl the selv st, *p1, k1*, rep from * to * to end of row, purl the selv st.

Work the sts at the transition between the long sides and the center part somewhat tighter to create a neat transition.

Continue in pattern, working a total of 54 (60/60/68/68) rows.

Continue as listed for the size worked:

Row 55 (RS): Selv st, knit 30 sts in pattern, sl1-k2tog-psso (slip the 1st st knitwise, knit the 2nd and 3rd sts together, pass the slipped st over), knit 5 sts in pattern, sl2-k2tog-psso (slip the 1st and 2nd sts knitwise, insert the left needle from front to back into both sts, knit both sts together, place the 3rd knit st and the st resulting from having knitted together the 2 sts back onto the left needle, pass the 3rd st over the st resulting from having knitted together the 2 sts), knit 30 sts in pattern, selv st [= 69 sts].

Rows 56–60: Work in pattern.

Sizes S (M/L):

Row 61: Selv st, knit 28 (30/30) sts in pattern, sl1-k2tog-psso (as described in Row 55), knit 5 sts in pattern, sl2-k2tog-psso (as described in Row 55), knit 28 (30/30) sts in pattern, selv st [= 65 (69/69) sts].

Rows 62–68: Work in pattern.

All sizes:

Row 69: Selv st, knit 26 (28/28/30/30) sts in pattern, sl1-k2tog-psso (as described in Row 55), knit 5 sts in pattern, sl2-k2tog-psso (as described in Row 55), knit 26 (28/28/30/30) sts in pattern, selv st [= 61 (65/65/69/69) sts].

Rows 70–76: Work in pattern, break the working yarn.

BACK SHAPING

Row 1 of the chart (WS): Join new working yarn in color Sand on the inside of the hood, and work a WS row as follows:

Slip 17 sts to the right needle, p27 (31/31/35/35), leave the remaining 17 sts on the left needle unworked.

Now, increases will be worked in every row as follows: Inc 1 st from the bar between sts either knitwise twisted or purlwise twisted, depending on the row worked (RS or WS). Slip markers in every row as you encounter them; in this section, the selv sts will be worked in pattern.

Row 1 (RS, Row 2 in the chart) in Sand: K2, place m, inc 1, k21 (25/25/29/29), inc 1, place m, k2 [= 29 (33/33/37/37) sts].

Row 2 (WS, Row 3 in the chart): P2 in Sand, inc 1 (Rosé), 1 st in Sand, p23 (27/27/31/31) sts in pattern, inc 1 (Sand), 1 st in Rosé, slip m, p2 in Sand [= 31 (35/35/39/39) sts].

Rep these 2 rows another 7 (9/11/11/13) times, continuing the colorwork pattern according to the chart and increasing 28 (36/44/44/52) sts in all [= 59 (71/79/83/91) sts].

Break the working yarn, and place the sts on a stitch holder, extra needle, or spare cord for holding.

KNITTING ON THE FRONTS

Hold the back with the right side of the fabric facing you, the previously held sts of the back pointing toward the bottom, and the cast-on edge located at the top.

RIGHT SHOULDER

In Rosé, pick up and knit 16 (20/24/24/28) sts along the edge of the right shoulder from the outermost corner of the shoulder to the hood.

Row 1 (WS) in Rosé: Sl1, p15 (19/23/23/27).

Row 2 (RS) in Rosé: K15 (19/23/23/27), ssk the last shoulder st together with the 1st st of the formerly held hood st (with the last shoulder st on top) [= 16 (20/24/24/28) sts].

Row 3 (WS, Row 8 of the chart): Sl1, p15 (19/23/23/27) in pattern.

Work Rows 2 and 3 a total of 7 times, continuing the pattern (= 14 rows) [right front = 16 (20/24/24/28) sts].

Break the working yarn, place the st on hold. If using a circular needle with long cord, the st can remain on the cord.

LEFT SHOULDER

In Rosé, pick up and knit 16 (20/24/24/28) sts along the edge of the left shoulder from the hood to the outermost corner of the shoulder.

Row 1 (WS) in Rosé: P15 (19/23/23/27), slip the last st.

Row 2 (RS) in Rosé: Ssk the 1st st of the hood together with the 1st st of the shoulder (shoulder st on top), k15 (19/23/23/27).

Row 3 (WS, Row 8 of the chart): P15 (19/23/23/27), slip the last st [= 16 (20/24/24/28) sts].

Work Rows 2 and 3 a total of 7 times, continuing the pattern (= 14 rows).

Row 18 (RS, Row 3 of the chart): Ssk the 1st st of the hood together with the 1st st of the shoulder, k2, M1R from the bar between sts (using the tip of the right needle, lift the bar between sts from back to front, and knit this strand through the back loop, twisted), k13 (17/21/21/25), ssk the last 2 sts (the next-to-last st on top) [left front = 16 (20/24/24/28) sts].

Leave the shoulder st on the needle.

SLEEVES

Pull the cord of the circular needle out between the sts into a loop and, for the left sleeve, in Sand, pick up and knit 12 (14/14/16/16) sts from the edge of the shoulder.

Place the sts of the back on the main needle again, immediately k2tog the 1st and the 2nd st (2nd st on top), work the sts of the back in pattern to the last 2 sts, ssk these sts (the next-to-last st on top) [back = 57 (69/77/81/89) sts].

Pull the cord of the circular needle into a loop again and pick up and knit 12 (14/14/16/16) sts for the right sleeve along the edge of the right shoulder.

Now, work the sts of the right front: k2tog the 1st and the 2nd st (2nd st on top), work in pattern to the last 3 sts. M1L from the bar between sts (lifting the bar with the left needle from front to back and knitting the loop through the back leg, twisted), k2, skp the last st of the front together with the next hood st [right front= 16 (20/24/24/28) sts].

Place markers as below, slipping markers in subsequent rows as you encounter them.

Row 16 (WS): Slip the 1st st, p15 (19/23/23/27) in pattern (right front), place m, p12 (14/14/16/16) in pattern (right sleeve), place m, p57 (69/77/81/89) in pattern (back), place m, p12 (14/14/16/16) in pattern (left sleeve), place m, p16 (20/24/24/28) in pattern (left front), p2 of the held hood sts, turn work [left front = 18 (22/26/26/30) sts].

The Main Pattern is continued, which will not be specially noted any more from here on.

Row 17 (RS) (begin to work German short rows):

Left front: Double st, k17 (21/25/25/29).

Left sleeve: 1st set of sleeve increases: inc 1 by working kfb, k10 (12/12/14/14), inc 1 [= 14 (16/16/18/18) sts].

Back: K57 (69/77/81/89).

Right sleeve: 1st set of sleeve increases: inc 1, k10 (12/12/14/14), inc 1 [= 14 (16/16/18/18) sts].

Right front: K16 (20/24/24/28), k2 of the held hood sts [= 18 (22/26/26/30) sts].

Row 18 (WS): Double st, purl to end of row, p2 of the held hood sts [left front = 20 (24/28/28/32) sts].

Row 19 (RS): Double st, k3, M1R from the bar between sts (twisted), k16 (20/24/24/28 = 21 (25/29/29/33) sts for the left front), 2nd set of sleeve increases: inc 1, k12 (14/14/16/16), inc 1 = 16 (18/18/20/20) sts, k57 (69/77/81/89), 2nd set of sleeve increases: inc 1, k12 (14/14/16/16), inc 1 = 16 (18/18/20/20) sts, k14 (18/22/22/26), M1R from the bar between sts (twisted), k4, k2 of the held hood sts [right front = 21 (25/29/29/33) sts].

Row 20 (WS): Double st, purl to end of row, p2 of the held hood sts [= 23 (27/31/31/35) sts for the left front].

Row 21 (RS): Double st, k22 (26/30/30/34), 3rd set of sleeve increases: inc 1, k14 (16/16/18/18), inc 1 = 18 (20/20/22/22) sts, k57 (69/77/81/89), 3rd set of sleeve increases: inc 1, k14 (16/16/18/18), inc 1 = 18 (20/20/22/22) sts, k21 (25/29/29/33), k2 of the held hood sts [right front = 23 (27/31/31/35) sts].

Row 22 (WS): Double st, purl to end of row, purl the last 3 sts of the hood [= 26/30/34/34/38 sts.]

Row 23 (RS): K26 (30/34/34/38), 4th set of sleeve increases as described before = 20 (22/22/24/24) sts, k57 (69/77/81/89), 4th set of sleeve increases as described before = 20 (22/22/24/24) sts, k23 (27/31/31/35), knit the last 3 sts of the hood [= 26 (30/34/34/38) sts].

Row 24 (WS): Purl all sts.

From here on, multiple instructions must be worked simultaneously. For this reason, first read through all the instructions before you proceed.

Continue working increases as described for the previous rows as listed for your size:

A little reminder:

M1L from the bar between sts = lifting the bar with the left needle from front to back and knitting the loop through the back leg, twisted

M1R from the bar between sts = lifting the bar with the right needle from back to front and knitting the loop through the back leg, twisted

Size S:

Continue increases in every other RS row, 7 times in all, then work 6 rows even without increases, *also* in every RS row, 4 times in all, from the beginning of the sleeve on, work k2, M1R from the bar between sts, work to last 2 sleeve sts, M1L from the bar between sts, k2 [= 42 sts].

Size M:

Continue increases in every other RS row, 9 times in all, then work 2 rows even without increases, *also* in every RS row, 4 times in all, from the beginning of the sleeve on, work k2, M1R from the bar between sts, work to last 2 sleeve sts, M1L from the bar between sts, k2 [= 48 sts].

Size L:

Continue increases once more in the following RS row, in every other RS row, 8 times in all, then work 6 rows even without increases, *also* in every RS row, 5 times in all, from the beginning of the sleeve on, work k2, M1R from the bar between sts, work to last 2 sleeve sts, M1L from the bar between sts, k2 [= 50 sts].

Continue increases in every RS row, 2 times more, in every other RS row, 8 times in all, then work 8 rows even without increases, *also* in every RS row, 5 times in all, from the beginning of the sleeve on, work k2, M1R from the bar between sts, work to last 2 sleeve sts, M1L from the bar between sts, k2 [= 54 sts].

Size XXL:

Continue increases in every RS row, 2 times more, in every other RS row, 8 times in all, then work 10 rows even without increases, *also* in every RS row, 5 times in all, from the beginning of the sleeve on, work k2, M1R from the bar between sts, work to last 2 sleeve sts, M1L from the bar between sts, k2 [= 54 sts].

AT THE SAME TIME, WORKING THE FRONT AND THE BACK

Increases are worked as follows for the respective size:

Left front: Work to the last 2 sts of the front, M1L from the bar between sts, k2.

Back: K2, M1R from the bar between sts, work to the last 2 sts of the back, M1L from the bar between sts, k2.

Right front: K2, M1R from the bar between sts, work the remaining sts of the front.

Size S:

Rows 1–28: Work in stockinette stitch.

Row 29: Work the 1st increase for the front as described above, then rep increases in every RS row 6 times more.

During Row 33: Additionally, work the 1st increase for the back as described above, then rep increase in every RS row, 4 times in all.

After having worked 42 rows, all increases for front and back have been completed. [front = 33 sts, back = 67 sts].

Size M:

Rows 1–32: Work in stockinette stitch.

Row 33: Work the 1st increase for the front as described above, then rep increases in every RS row 6 times more.

In Row 41: Additionally, work the 1st increase for the back as described above, then rep increase in every RS row, 2 times more.

After having worked 46 rows, all increases for front and back have been completed. [front = 37 sts, back = 73 sts].

Size L:

Rows 1–36: Work in stockinette stitch.

Row 37: Work the 1st increase for the front as described above, then rep increases in every RS row 6 times more.

In Row 45: Additionally, work the 1st increase for the back as described above, then rep increase in every RS row, 2 times more.

After having worked 50 rows, all increases for front and back have been completed [front = 41 sts, back = 81 sts].

Size XL:

Rows 1–36: Work in stockinette stitch.

Row 37: Work the 1st increase for the front as described above, then rep increases in every RS row, 8 times more.

In Row 49: Additionally, work the 1st increase for the back as described above, then rep increase in every RS row, 2 times more.

After having worked 54 rows, all increases for front and back have been completed [front = 43 sts, back = 85 sts].

Size XXL:

Rows 1–40: Work in stockinette stitch.

Row 41: Work the 1st increase for the front as described above, then rep increases in every RS row, 8 times more.

In Row 51: Additionally, work the 1st increase for the back as described above, then rep increase in every RS row, 3 times more.

After having worked 58 rows, all increases for front and back have been completed [front = 47 sts, back = 95 sts].

DIVIDING FOR THE SLEEVES

Knit the 33 (37/42/43/47) sts of the left front, transfer the 42 (48/50/54/54) sts of the left sleeve to a spare cord, extra needle, or piece of waste yarn for holding, cast on 6 (6/6/10/10) new underarm sts, knit the 67 (73/81/85/95) sts of the back, transfer the 42 (48/50/54/54) sts of the right sleeve to a spare cord, extra needle, or piece of waste yarn for holding, cast on 6 (6/6/10/10) new underarm sts, knit the 33 (37/42/43/47) sts of the right front [= 145 (159/177/191/209) sts].

Now, continue for approx. 11.8 in/30 cm in pattern; the last row is either a Row 5 or Row 10 of the chart.

HEM RIBBING

Work in the following manner:

Row 1: K3 in Sand, *k1 in Rosé, k1 in Sand*, rep from * to * 69 (76/85/92/101) times, k1 in Rosé, k3 in Sand.

Row 2: Purl all sts in the same color sequence as before.

Work these 2 rows a total of 6 times = 12 rows, break the working yarn in Sand.

Then, bind off the stitches in Rosé using the Italian bind-off (see instructions in Basics chapter on pages 22–23), after having worked 2 setup rows as follows:

Row 1: K1, *k1, slip 1 purlwise with yarn in front of work*, rep from * to * continuously, k2.

Row 2: P1, *slip 1 purlwise with yarn in back of work, p1*, rep from * to * continuously, p1.

Bind off all sts using Italian bind-off.

SLEEVES

Take up the formerly held 42 (48/50/54/54) sleeve sts, place them on a spare needle and pick up and knit 6 (6/6/10/10) sts from the armhole edge on the body (placing a marker to indicate the BOR after half of the sts), and join into the round, continuing the pattern sequence [= 48 (54/56/64/64 sts].

Sleeve tapering decreases are worked as follows:

Beginning in the middle of the sleeve (at the marker): K1, k2tog, work sleeve sts to the last 3 sts of the round, skp, k1 [= 2 sts decreased in each round].

Now, work these decreases as follows:

TIP

At the corner of the armhole edge, always pick up and knit an additional st. This prevents unsightly holes. Decrease this additionally picked-up st in the following round by knitting it together with either the st before it or the st after it.

Size S:

In every 5th round, 10 times in all (28 sts).

Size M/L:

In every 4th round, 8 times in all, then in every 6th round, 3 times in all (32/34 sts).

Size XL/XXL:

In every 4th round, 10 times in all, then in every 5th round, 2 times in all (44 sts).

CUFF RIBBING

Work in the following manner:

Row 1: K3 in Sand, *k1 in Rosé, k1 in Sand*, rep from * to * 69 (76/85/92/101) times, k1 in Rosé, k3 in Sand.

Row 2: Purl all sts in the same color sequence as before.

Work these 2 rows a total of 7 times = 14 rows.

Bind off all sts knitwise in color sequence.

BUTTONHOLE BAND

Along the edge of the left front, pick up and knit 99 (104/109/113/117) sts in Rosé.

WS row: Purl selv st in Rosé, *p1 in Sand, p1 in Rosé*, rep from * to * 48 (51/53/55/57) times, p1 in Sand, purl selv st in Rosé.

Rows 1–8: Work sts in stockinette stitch in color sequence, then bind off all sts knitwise in color sequence.

Along the edge of the right front, pick up and knit 101 (105/109/113/117) sts in Rosé.

WS row: Purl selv st in Rosé, *p1 in Sand, p1 in Rosé*, rep from * to * 49 (51/53/55/57) times, p1 in Sand, purl selv st in Rosé.

Rows 1–4: Work sts in stockinette stitch in color sequence.

Row 5: Work a total of 5 buttonholes in this row as follows: Selv st, 4 sts in pattern, *bind off 4 sts in pattern (1st buttonhole), 18 (19/20/21/22) sts in pattern*, rep from * to * 3 times more, bind off 4 sts in pattern (5th buttonhole), 3 sts in pattern, selv st.

Row 6: Work all sts in pattern, above each buttonhole, using both strands of working yarn held together, cast on 4 new sts.

Rows 7–8: Work sts in stockinette stitch in color sequence, then bind off all sts knitwise in color sequence.

FINISHING

Sew the 5 buttons to the left front opposite the buttonholes.

Carefully weave in all ends, wash the cardigan according to the manufacturer's washing instructions on the ball band of the yarn, pull it into shape, and let it dry spread out flat on an even horizontal surface.

CHART

The chart is worked as stated in the instructions and continuously repeated heightwise.

CHARA
Short Jacket

◆◆◆

SIZES

S (M/L/XL)

Chest Circumference

35.5 (39.5/43.25/47.25) in/90 (100/110/120) cm

Length from Underarm

11 in/28 cm

Total Length

20.9 in/53 cm

MATERIALS

- Lang Yarns Mohair Luxe; DK weight; 77% mohair, 23% silk; 191.25 yd/175 m per 0.9 oz/25 g

  Bordeaux 0180: 3 (4/5/6) skeins

  Stone 0096: 3 (4/5/6) skeins

- Lang Yarns Merino 400 Lace; sock/baby weight; 100% extra fine merino wool; 219 yd/200 m per 0.9 oz/25 g

  Bordeaux 0066: 3 (4/5/6) skeins

  Stone 0096: 3 (4/5/6) skeins

- Five approx. 0.7 in/18 mm gray buttons
- US size 7 (4.5 mm) circular knitting needles in different lengths
- Stitch markers
- Tapestry needle
- Scissors

GAUGE

In pattern: 22 sts and 24/25 rows = 4 x 4 in/10 x 10 cm

STITCH PATTERNS

Main Pattern

Stockinette stitch in charted colorwork pattern in the indicated order of work.

Ribbing Pattern for Collar and Buttonhole and Button Bands

Row 1: *K2, p2*, rep from * to * continuously.

Row 2: Work all sts as they appear, knitting the knits and purling the purls.

Rep these 2 rows as stated in the instructions.

Ribbing Pattern for Body and Sleeves

Row 1: *K2 in Stone, p2 in Bordeaux *, rep from * to * continuously.

Row 2: Work the sts in color sequence as they appear (knitting the knits and purling the purls).

Rep these 2 rows as stated in the instructions.

Increases

Please refer to illustrated tutorial in Basics chapter on pages 17–18.

INSTRUCTIONS

Always work with 1 strand Mohair Luxe held together with 1 strand of Merino 400 Lace in the same color.

BACK

RIGHT SHOULDER

Cast on 20 (26/32/38) sts in Stone.

Rows 1 (RS) and 2 (WS): Selv st in Stone, work the pattern repeat (6 sts wide) 3 (4/5/6) times widthwise, selv st in Stone.

Row 3: Selv st in Stone, work the pattern repeat (6 sts wide) 3 (4/5/6) times widthwise, inc 1 in pattern, selv st in Stone [= 21 (27/33/39) sts].

Row 4: Work a WS row according to the charted pattern.

Row 5: Selv st in Stone, work the pattern repeat (6 sts wide) 3 (4/5/6) times widthwise, work sts #1+2 of the pattern repeat, cast on 2 new sts [= 23 (29/35/41) sts].

Row 6: Work a WS row according to the charted pattern.

Row 7: Selv st in Stone, work the pattern repeat (6 sts wide) 3 (4/5/6) times widthwise, work sts #1–4 of the pattern repeat, cast on 40 new sts [= 63 (69/75/81) sts.

Transfer the sts to a stitch holder or piece of waste yarn for holding.

LEFT SHOULDER

Work mirror-inverted to the right shoulder, up to Row 6 [= 23 (29/35/41) sts].

In Row 7, join the live sts of both shoulders by knitting left shoulder sts, 40 new sts, and right shoulder sts into 1 row [= 86 (98/110/122) sts].

Continue working even, working the pattern repeat heightwise 3.5 (4/4.5/5) times = 28 (32/36/40) rows.

ARMHOLE INCREASES

Row 1: Selv st, inc 1, work the pattern repeat 14 (16/18/20) times widthwise, inc 1, selv st [= 88 (100/112/124) sts].

Row 2: Work in established pattern.

Row 3: Selv st, inc 1, work st #6 of the pattern repeat, work the pattern repeat 14 (16/18/20) times widthwise, work st #1 of the pattern repeat, inc 1, selv st [= 90 (102/114/126) sts].

Row 4: Work in established pattern.

Row 5: Selv st, inc 1, work sts #5+6 of the pattern repeat, work the pattern repeat 14 (16/18/20) times widthwise, work sts #1–2 of the pattern repeat, inc 1, selv st [= 92 (104/116/128) sts].

Row 6: Work in established pattern.

Row 7: Cast on 3 new sts, work sts #4–6 of the pattern repeat, work the pattern repeat 14 (16/18/20) times widthwise, work sts #1–4 of the pattern repeat, cast on 3 new sts [= 98 (110/122/134) sts].

Row 8: Work in established pattern.

Place the sts of the back on hold.

KNITTING ON THE FRONTS

RIGHT FRONT

In Stone, starting at the right edge of the shoulder, pick up and knit 20 (26/32/38) sts into the CO sts in the same pattern sequence as for the back.

At the same time, on the left edge, in every other row (RS), cast on 1 st 3 times, 2 sts 2 times, 3 sts once, 4 sts once, 9 sts once [= 43 (49/55/61) sts].

Work an additional 20 (24/28/32) rows in pattern.

Now, at the same height level as on the back, work armhole shaping increases [= 49 (55/61/67) sts].

LEFT FRONT

In Stone, starting at the left edge of the shoulder, pick up and knit 20 (26/32/38) sts into the CO sts in the same pattern sequence as for the back and work through armhole shaping increases mirror-inverted to the right front.

JOINING BACK AND FRONTS

In the next row, work the 49 (55/61/67) sts of the left front in established pattern, cast on 4 new underarm sts, work the next 98 (110/122/134) sts of the back in established pattern, cast on 4 new underarm sts, work the 49 (55/61/67) sts of the right front in established pattern [= 204 (228/252/276) sts].

The selv sts before and after the underarm sts are incorporated into the colorwork pattern and, together with the underarm sts, comprise a complete pattern repeat.

Work 9 in/23 cm more in pattern, ending with a Row 8 of the chart.

WELT

Work 6 rows in Stone in stockinette stitch.

In the next row, knit together every st with the corresponding st 6 rows below.

Purl 1 WS row in Stone.

CORRUGATED RIBBING

Row 1: Selv st in Stone, *k2 in Stone, p2 in Bordeaux*, rep from * to * 50 (56/62/68) times, k2 in Stone, selv st in Stone.

Row 2: Selv st in Stone, *k2 in Bordeaux, p2 in Stone*, rep from * to * 50 (56/62/68) times, k2 in Bordeaux, selv st in Stone.

Rows 3–10: Rep Rows 2 and 3.

Then, bind off all sts knitwise in Stone.

SLEEVES

Pick up and knit 84 (90/96/102) sts in Bordeaux around the armhole, beginning in the middle of the underarm sts at the side of the body.

Row 1: Transfer 37 (40/43/46) sts to a spare cord for holding without working them, work 9 sts in pattern (1 full pattern repeat +sts #1–3 of the pattern repeat once), transfer 38 (41/44/47) sts to a spare cord for holding without working them. Turn work.

Row 2: Double stitch (see page 21), 8 sts in pattern, incorporate 2 sts of the previously held sts and work them in pattern [= 11 sts].

Row 3: Double st, 10 sts in pattern, incorporate 2 sts of the previously held sts and work them in pattern [= 13 sts].

Rep Rows 2 and 3 another 16 (17/19/29) times in the same manner, always incorporating the sts increased at the sides into the stitch pattern.

Rep Rows 2 and 3 another 3 (4/3/4) times in the same manner, however, only incorporating 1 st each time; 1 st remains, incorporate this last st into the stitch pattern during the last row [= 84 (90/96/102) sts].

Continue working in the round, working a total of 8 in/20 cm, ending with a Row 8 of the pattern repeat.

WELT

Work 6 rows in Stone in stockinette stitch.

In the next row, knit together every st with the corresponding st 6 rows below.

Purl 1 WS row in Stone, while decreasing a total of 10 (8/10/8) sts evenly spaced by working p2tog [= 74 (82/86/94) sts].

CORRUGATED RIBBING

Rnds 1–10: *K2 in Stone, p2 in Bordeaux*, rep from * to * 18 (20/21/23) times, k2 in Stone.

Then, bind off all sts knitwise in Stone.

BUTTONHOLE AND BUTTON BANDS

RIGHT FRONT BAND

In Bordeaux, pick up and knit 92 sts from the front edge of the right front.

Row 1 (WS): P1 (selv st), *p2, k2*, rep from * to * 22 times, p2, selv st.

Rows 2–5: Work all sts as they appear.

Row 6: K1 (selv st), work 5 sts in established pattern, for the 1st buttonhole, bind off 2 sts without working them, immediately cast on 2 new sts, *18 sts in established pattern, buttonhole*, rep from * to * 4 times, work 5 sts in established pattern, knit the selv st.

Rows 7–9: Work all sts as they appear. Incorporate the sts above the buttonhole into the stitch pattern.

Bind off all sts knitwise.

LEFT FRONT BAND

Work mirror-inverted to right front band, but without buttonholes.

COLLAR

In Bordeaux, pick up and knit 120 sts around the neckline edge (31 sts for each front and 58 sts on the back), except for the buttonhole band.

Row 1: P1 (selv st), *p2, k2*, rep from * to * 29 times, p2, purl the selv st.

Rows 2–9: Work all sts as they appear.

Bind off all sts knitwise.

FINISHING

Weave in all ends neatly. Sew on the buttons. Cover the cardigan with wet cloths and let it dry spread out flat on an even horizontal surface.

CHART

KENDRA
Pullover with elongated raglan

SIZES

S (M/L/XL)

Chest Circumference

39.5 (43.25/47.25/51.25) in/100 (110/120/130) cm
(includes positive ease of + 4 in/10 cm)

Length from Underarm

13.75 in/35 cm

Total Length

24.5 in/62 cm

MATERIALS

- Lang Yarns Mohair Luxe; DK weight; 77% mohair, 23% silk; 191.25 yd/175 m per 0.9 oz/25 g skein

  Petrol 0188: 3 (4/5/6) skeins

  Off White 0094: 3 (4/5/6) skeins

- Lang Yarns Merino 400 Lace; sock/baby weight; 100% extra fine merino wool; 219 yd/200 m per 0.9 oz/25 g skein

  Petrol 0088: 3 (4/5/6) skeins

  Off White 0094: 3 (4/5/6) skeins

- US size 6 (4.0 mm) and size 7 (4.5 mm) circular knitting needles in different lengths

- US size 7 (4.5 mm) double-pointed needle set for sleeves, if desired

- US size G-6 (4.0 mm) crochet hook

- A scrap piece of cotton yarn for the provisional cast-on

- Stitch markers

- Tapestry needle

- Scissors

GAUGE

In pattern on US 7 (4.5 mm) needles: 24 sts and 23 rows = 4 x 4 in/10 x 10 cm

STITCH PATTERNS

Main Pattern

Stockinette stitch in charted colorwork pattern in the indicated order of work.

The charted pattern repeat is 4 sts in width and 13 rows in height; repeat continuously as stated in the instructions.

Ribbing Pattern

Rnd 1: *K1 in White, p1 in Petrol*, rep from * to * continuously.

Rnd 2: *K1 in White, p1 in White*, rep from * to * continuously.

Raglan Stitches

Work 1 knit st in Rnds 1–7 and in Rnds 9–12, 1 st in Petrol in Rnds 8 and 13.

Short Rows

Please refer to illustrated tutorial in Basics chapter on page 21.

Increases

Please refer to illustrated tutorial in Basics chapter on pages 17–18.

INSTRUCTIONS

Kendra is worked top down in an elongated raglan construction.

Always work with 1 strand of Mohair Luxe in Petrol held together with 1 strand of Merino 400 Lace in Petrol, and with 1 strand of Mohair Luxe in Off White always held together with 1 strand of Merino 400 Lace in Off White.

TIP

Before you start, wind the 2 strands of Mohair and Merino in the same color together into 1 skein.

COLLAR

Cast on using the provisional cast-on method as follows:

Using a separate piece of waste yarn and a crochet hook, crochet a chain of 118, break yarn, and pull the yarn tail through the last chain to secure.

Flip the crocheted chain over so the bumps in back of the chain are facing you. Using knitting needles and the working yarn in Petrol, pick up and knit 108 sts as follows:

Skip the 1st 5 crocheted chains, insert the needle into the back bump of the next crocheted chain, and pull the working yarn through to create a st. Pick up and knit 107 sts more in this manner, skip the last 5 crocheted chains, and join into the round, placing a marker to indicate the BOR (center back).

Work 18 rnds in Ribbing Pattern. During the last round, divide work into sections for front/back and sleeves as follows:

Starting at the BOR: 20 sts for the 1st half of the back, place m, 1 Rg-st, place m, 12 sts for the right sleeve, place m, 1 Rg-st, place m, 40 sts for the front, place m, 1 Rg-st, place m, 12 sts for the left sleeve, place m, 1 Rg-st, place m, 20 sts for the 2nd half of the back.

Break the working yarn in Petrol.

SHAPING THE BACK NECKLINE WITH SHORT ROWS

This part is worked in Off White, and markers are slipped as you encounter them. Remove the BOR marker in the back.

Row 1: K20, M1R from the bar between sts (twisted), k1 (Rg-st), M1R from the bar between sts (twisted), k12, M1R from the bar between sts (twisted), k1 (Rg-st), M1R from the bar between sts (twisted), k1, turn work.

Row 2: Double st, p1, p1 (Rg-st), p14, p1 (Rg-st), p41, M1L from the bar between sts (twisted), p1 (Rg-st), M1L from the bar between sts (twisted), p12, M1L from the bar between sts (twisted), p1 (Rg-st), M1L from the bar between sts (twisted), p1, turn work.

Row 3: Double st, k1, k1 (Rg-st), k14, k1 (Rg-st), k42, M1R from the bar between sts (twisted), k1 (Rg-st), M1R from the bar between sts (twisted), k14, M1R from the bar between sts (twisted), k1 (Rg-st), M1R from the bar between sts (twisted), k4, turn work.

Row 4: Double st, p4, p1 (Rg-st), p16, p1 (Rg-st), p43, M1L from the bar between sts (twisted), p1 (Rg-st), M1L from the bar between sts (twisted), p14, M1L from the bar between sts (twisted), p1 (Rg-st), M1L from the bar between sts (twisted), p4, turn work.

Row 5: Double st, k4, k1 (Rg-st), k16, k1 (Rg-st), k44, k1 (Rg-st), k16, 1 Rg-st.

In this spot, place a marker in a different color to mark the new BOR at the raglan line on the right front.

RAGLAN LINES AND BEGINNING OF MAIN PATTERN

Raglan line increases are always worked in the appropriate color of the pattern; after the Rg-sts, the pattern repeat is read from left to right; before the Rg-sts, the pattern repeat is read from right to left.

Rnd 1 (Row 8 of the chart) in Petrol: 1 Rg-st, inc 1 = st #2 of the pattern repeat, work sts #3+4 of the pattern repeat once, work the pattern repeat (4 sts in width) 10 times widthwise, work sts #1+2 of the pattern repeat once, inc 1 = st #3 of the pattern repeat, 1 Rg-st, inc 1 = st #2 of the pattern repeat, work sts #3+4 of the pattern repeat once, work the pattern repeat (4 sts in width) 3 times widthwise, work sts #1+2 of the pattern repeat once, inc 1 = st #3 of the pattern repeat, 1 Rg-st, inc 1 = st #2 of the pattern repeat, work sts #3+4 of the pattern repeat once, work the pattern repeat (4 sts in width) 10 times widthwise, work sts #1+2 of the pattern repeat once, inc 1 = st #3 of the pattern repeat, 1 Rg-st, inc 1 = st #2 of the pattern repeat, work sts #3+4 of the pattern repeat once, work the pattern repeat (4 sts in width) 3 times widthwise, work sts #1+2 of the pattern repeat once, inc 1 = st #3 of the pattern repeat [= 132 sts].

Now, continue the pattern according to the chart, and work raglan increases in every other round another 37 (41/45/49) times for front and back, and 33 (37/41/45) times for the sleeves. As a result, after having

completed all raglan increases, you will end up with full pattern repeats before and after the raglan lines and will have a total of 120 (128/136/144) sts each for the front and back, and 84 (92/100/108) sts for each sleeve.

DIVIDING THE SLEEVES FROM THE BODY

Continuing to work in Main Pattern, slip the 1st st, work 118 (126/134/142) sts (front), knit 1 st and the raglan st together working skp, transfer the 84 (92/100/108) sts of the left sleeve to waste yarn or a spare cord (note the row of the pattern repeat worked last), with 2 strands of yarn held together, cast on 4 (4/8/12) new underarm sts, knit the raglan st together with the next knit st of the back by working k2tog, work 118 (126/134/142) sts (back), knit 1 st and the raglan st together working skp, transfer the 84 (92/100/108) sts of the right sleeve to waste yarn or a spare cord, with 2 strands of yarn held together, cast on 4 (4/8/12) new underarm sts (placing a new BOR marker after the 2nd stitch), knit the raglan st together with the next knit st of the front by working k2tog [= 248 (264/288/312) sts].

The underarm sts yield 1 (1/2/3) full pattern repeat(s) and need to be incorporated into the appropriate round of the Main Pattern.

Continue in Main Pattern until approx. 21.7 in/55 cm have been worked (measured in the back, not counting the collar) = Chart Rows 8–13 once and 10 complete heightwise pattern repeats of the chart. During the last round, decrease 24 sts evenly spaced (by working skp) [= 224 (240/264/288) sts].

HEM RIBBING

Using US 6 (4.0 mm) needles, work 15 rnds in Ribbing Pattern, then bind off all sts knitwise in Off White.

SLEEVES

Take up the formerly held 84 (92/100/108) sleeve sts, place them on a spare needle, pick up and knit 4 (4/8/12) sts from the underarm sts of the body, placing a marker to indicate the BOR after half of the sts, join into the round, and continue in Main Pattern in the established manner, finishing with a Row 7 (2/10/5) of the chart [= 88 (96/108/120) sts].

Then, work another 13.8 in/35 cm in Main Pattern, while working sleeve tapering decreases in the rnds indicated for your size as follows:

Size S:

12 decreases per rnd in Rnds 6 and 12.

Size M:

15 decreases per rnd in Rnds 2, 7, and 12.

Size L:

18 decreases per rnd in Rnds 2, 7, and 12.

Size XL:

20 decreases per rnd in Rnds 2, 7, and 13.

Work Decrease Rnd as follows, beginning at the BOR marker: slip marker, k2, k2tog, work to last 4 sts before BOR marker, skp, k2 = 24 (30/36/40) sts decreased in all [= 64 (66/72/80) sts].

At this point, sleeve length can be adjusted to personal preferences, the last round worked should either be a Row 7 or 13 of the chart.

In Off White, knit 1 rnd and decrease 8 sts evenly spaced (by working ssk) [= 56 (58/64/72) sts].

Then, bind off all sts using applied I-cord bind-off in either Off White or Petrol (see instructions in Basics chapter on pages 24–25).

COLLAR FINISHING

Dissolve the provisional cast-on sts one by one and place the live sts onto a circular needle of appropriate cord length. Work applied I-cord bind-off in Petrol.

FINISHING

Carefully weave in all ends. Spread out the sweater flat on an even surface, pull it into shape, cover it with wet cloths, and let it dry.

CHART

KEELA
Turtleneck with elongated raglan

SIZES

S (M/L/XL)

Chest Circumference

39.5 (43.25/47.25/51.25) in/100 (110/120/130) cm
(includes positive ease of + 4 in/10 cm)

Length from Underarm

Approx. 13.8 in/35 cm – adjustable

Total Length

Approx. 23.6 in/60 cm

MATERIALS

- Lang Yarns Mohair Luxe; DK weight; 77% mohair, 23% silk; 191.25 yd/175 m per 0.9 oz/25 g skein

  Vintage Pink 0348: 3 (4/5/6) skeins

  Off White 0094: 3 (4/5/6) skeins

- Lang Yarns Merino 400 Lace; sock/baby weight; 100% merino wool extra fine; 219 yd/200 m per 0.9 oz/25 g skein

  Vintage Pink 0048: 3 (4/5/6) skeins

  Off White 0094: 3 (4/5/6) skeins

- US size 6 (4.0 mm) and US 7 (4.5 mm) circular knitting needles in different lengths

- US size 7 (4.5 mm) double-pointed needle set for sleeves

- Stitch markers

- Tapestry needle

- Scissors

GAUGE

In pattern on US 7 (4.5 mm) needles: 24 sts and 23 rows = 4 x 4 in/10 x 10 cm

STITCH PATTERNS

Main Pattern

Stockinette stitch in charted colorwork pattern in the indicated order of work.

Ribbing Pattern

In rnds: *K1, p1* rep from * to * continuously in the indicated color.

Raglan Stitch

1 st in Off White in Rnds 1–7 and Rnds 9–12, 1 st in Vintage Pink in Rnds 8 and 13.

Short Rows

Please refer to illustrated tutorial in Basics chapter on page 21.

Increases

Please refer to illustrated tutorial in Basics chapter on pages 17–18.

INSTRUCTIONS

Keela is worked top down in an elongated raglan construction.

Always work with 1 strand of Mohair Luxe in Vintage Pink held together with 1 strand of Merino 400 Lace in Vintage Pink, and with 1 strand Mohair Luxe in Off White always held together with 1 strand of Merino 400 Lace in Off White.

TIP

Before you start, wind the 2 strands of Mohair and Merino in the same color together into 1 skein.

Using US 7 (4.5 mm) needles and Off White, cast on 108 sts, and join work into the round, taking care not to twist the cast-on row.

Then, knit 1 round while placing markers as follows: 20 sts for the 1st half of the back, place m, 1 Rg-st, place m, 12 sts for the right sleeve, place m, 1 Rg-st, place m, 40 sts for the front, place m, 1 Rg-st, place m, 12 sts for the left sleeve, place m, 1 Rg-st, place m, 20 sts for the 2nd half of the back.

SHAPING THE BACK NECKLINE WITH SHORT ROWS

This part is worked in Off White and markers are slipped as you encounter them.

Row 1: K20, M1R from the bar between sts (twisted), 1 Rg-st, M1R from the bar between sts (twisted), k12, M1R from the bar between sts (twisted), 1 Rg-st, M1R from the bar between sts (twisted), k1, turn work.

Row 2: Double st, p1, p1 (Rg-st), p14, p1 (Rg-st), p41, M1L from the bar between sts (twisted), p1 (Rg-st), M1L from the bar between sts (twisted), p12, M1L from the bar between sts (twisted), p1 (Rg-st), M1L from the bar between sts (twisted), p1, turn work.

Row 3: Double st, k1, k1 (Rg-st), k14, k1 (Rg-st), k42, M1R from the bar between sts (twisted), 1 Rg-st, M1R from the bar between sts (twisted), k14, M1R from the bar between sts (twisted), k1 (Rg-st), M1R from the bar between sts (twisted), k4, turn work.

Row 4: Double st, p4, p1 (Rg-st), p16, p1 (Rg-st), p43, M1L from the bar between sts (twisted), 1 Rg-st, M1L from the bar between sts (twisted), p14, M1L from the bar between sts (twisted), p1 (Rg-st), M1L from the bar between sts (twisted), p4, turn work.

Row 5: Double st, k4, k1 (Rg-st), k16, k1 (Rg-st), k44, k1 (Rg-st), k16, 1 Rg-st.

In this spot, place a marker in a different color for the new BOR here at the raglan line on the right front.

RAGLAN LINES AND BEGINNING OF MAIN PATTERN

Raglan line increases are always worked in the appropriate color of the pattern; after the Rg-sts, the pattern repeat is read from left to right; before the Rg-sts, the pattern repeat is read from right to left.

Row 1 (Row 8 of the chart) in Vintage Pink: 1 Rg-st, inc 1 = st #2 of the pattern repeat, work sts #3+4 of the pattern repeat once, work the pattern repeat (4 sts in width) 10 times widthwise, work sts #1+2 of the pattern repeat once, inc 1 = st #3 of the pattern repeat, 1 Rg-st, inc 1 = st #2 of the pattern repeat, work sts #3+4 of the pattern repeat once, work the pattern repeat (4 sts in width) 3 times widthwise, work sts #1+2 of the pattern repeat once, inc 1 = st #3 of the pattern repeat, 1 Rg-st, inc 1 = st #2 of the pattern repeat, work sts #3+4 of the pattern repeat once, work the pattern repeat (4 sts in width) 10 times widthwise, work sts #1+2 of the pattern repeat once, inc 1 = st #3 of the pattern repeat, 1 Rg-st, inc 1 = st #2 of the pattern repeat, work sts #3+4 of the pattern repeat once, work the pattern repeat (4 sts in width) 3 times widthwise, work sts #1+2 of the pattern repeat once, inc 1 = st #3 of the pattern repeat [= 132 sts].

Now, continue the pattern according to the chart, and work raglan increases another 37 (41/45/49) times for front and back, and 33 (37/41/45) times for the sleeves in every other round. As a result, after having completed the raglan increases, you will end up with full pattern repeats before and after the raglan lines and will have a total of 120 (128/136/144) sts each for the front and back and 84 (92/100/108) sts for each sleeve.

DIVIDING THE SLEEVES FROM THE BODY

Continuing to work in Main Pattern, slip the 1st st, work 118 (126/134/142) sts (front), knit 1 st and the raglan st together working skp, transfer the 84 (92/100/108) sts of the left sleeve to waste yarn or a spare cord (note the row of the pattern repeat worked last). With 2 strands of yarn held together, cast on 4 (4/8/12) new underarm sts, knit the raglan st together with the next st of the back by working k2tog, work 118 (126/134/142) sts (back), knit 1 st and the raglan st together working skp, transfer the 84 (92/100/108) sts of the right sleeve to waste yarn or a spare cord, with 2 strands of yarn held together, cast on 4 (4/8/12) new underarm sts (placing a new BOR marker after the 2nd stitch), knit the raglan st together with the next st of the front by working k2tog [= 248 (264/288/312) sts].

The underarm sts yield 1 (1/2/3) full pattern repeat(s) and need to be incorporated into the appropriate round of the Main Pattern.

Continue in Main Pattern until approx. 21.7 in/55 cm have been worked (measured in the back, not counting the collar) = Chart Rows 8–13 once and 10 complete heightwise pattern repeats of the chart. During the last rnd, decrease 24 sts evenly spaced (by working skp) [= 224 (240/264/288) sts].

HEM RIBBING

Using US 6 (4.0 mm) needles, work 15 rnds in Off White in Hem Ribbing pattern, work 2 more rounds in Vintage Pink, then bind off all sts knitwise in Vintage Pink.

SLEEVES

Take up the formerly held 84 (92/100/108) sleeve sts, place them on a spare needle, pick up and knit 4 (4/8/12) sts from the underarm sts of the body, placing a marker to indicate the BOR after half of the sts, join into the round, and continue in Main Pattern in the established manner, finishing with a Row 7 (2/10/5) of the chart [= 88 (96/108/120) sts].

Then, work another 2.8 in/7 cm in Main Pattern, while working sleeve tapering decreases in Rnds 2, 7, and 13 of the Chart pattern repeat a total of 9 times as follows:

Starting at the beginning of the rnd: slip marker, k2, k2tog, work to last 4 sts before BOR marker, skp, k2 = 18 sts decreased in all [= 70 (78/90/102) sts].

At this point, sleeve length can be adjusted to personal preferences; the last round worked should either be a Rnd 7 or Rnd 13 of the chart.

Work 1 rnd in Off White: *K3, skp*, repeat from * to * 14 (15/18/20) times, (0 (3/0/4) sts remaining) [= 56 (63/72/82) sts].

Now, work 2 more rounds in Off White in Ribbing Pattern, then bind off all sts knitwise.

COLLAR

Using US 6 (4.0 mm) needles and Vintage Pink, pick up and knit 96 sts around the neckline edge. Beginning at the end of the back, place a marker to indicate the beginning of the rnd and work 2 rnds in Ribbing Pattern. Then, change to US 7 (4.5 mm) needles and work a total of 8 in/20 cm in Ribbing Pattern, then bind off all sts loosely in pattern.

FINISHING

Carefully weave in all ends. Spread the sweater flat on an even surface, pull it into shape, cover it with wet cloths, and let it dry.

CHART

The knitting chart is worked as stated in the instructions and continuously repeated heightwise.

MAISIE
Pullover with elongated raglan

◆◆◆

SIZES

S (M/L/XL)

Chest Circumference

41.25 (45.25/47.25/53) in/105 (115/125/135) cm
(includes positive ease of + 4 in/10 cm)

Length from Underarm

Approx. 14.5 in/37 cm (adjustable)

Total Length

Approx. 26 in/66 cm

MATERIALS

- Lang Yarns Mohair Luxe; DK weight; 77% mohair, 23% silk; 191.25 yd/175 m per 0.9 oz/25 g skein

  White 0001: 4 (4/5/6) skeins

  Lilac 0190: 2 (3/3/4) skeins

  Pink 0148: 1 (1/1/1) skein

- Lang Yarns Merino 400 Lace; 100% merino wool extra fine; 219 yd/200 m per 0.9 oz/25 g skein

  White 0094: 4 (4/5/6) skeins

  Lilac 0066: 2 (2/3/4) skeins

  Pink 0019: 1 (1/1/1) skein

- US size 6 (4.0 mm) circular knitting needles in different lengths

- US size 6 (4.0 mm) double-pointed needle set for sleeves, if desired

- US size G-6 (4.0 mm) crochet hook

- A length of scrap cotton yarn for the provisional cast-on

- Stitch markers

- Tapestry needle

- Scissors

GAUGE

In pattern: 24 sts and 30 rows = 4 x 4 in/10 x 10 cm

STITCH PATTERNS

Main Pattern

Stockinette stitch in charted colorwork pattern in the indicated order of work.

Color Sequence for Working in the Round

Work the Chart 1 pattern repeat (6 rows in height) 3 times heightwise in contrasting color Lilac (= Rnds 1–18 in White/Lilac), work 1 full pattern repeat in contrasting color Pink (= Rnds 19–24 in White/Pink) = 24 rounds, rep from * to * a total of 6 times.

Ribbing Pattern

In rounds: *K1 in White, k1 in Lilac*, rep from * to * continuously.

Raglan Stitches

Work 1 st in the appropriate contrasting color as stated (either Pink or Lilac).

Short Rows

Please refer to illustrated tutorial in Basics chapter on page 21.

Increases

Please refer to illustrated tutorial in Basics chapter on pages 17–18.

INSTRUCTIONS

Cast on using the provisional cast-on method as follows:

Using a separate piece of waste yarn and a crochet hook, crochet a chain of 120, break the working yarn, and pull the yarn tail through the last chain to secure.

Flip the crocheted chain over so the bumps in back of the chain are facing you. Using knitting needles and working yarn in color Lilac, pick up and knit 112 sts as follows:

Skip the 1st 4 crocheted chains, insert the needle into the back bump of the next crocheted chain, and pull the working yarn through to create a st. Pick up and knit 111 sts more in this manner, skip the last 4 crocheted chains, and join into the round, placing a marker to indicate the BOR (center back).

Work 18 rnds in Ribbing Pattern. During the last rnd, divide work into sections for front/back and sleeves as follows:

Starting at the BOR:

21 sts for the 1st half of the back, place m, 1 Rg-st, place m, 12 sts for the right sleeve, place m, 1 Rg-st, place m, 42 sts for the front, place m, 1 Rg-st, place m, 12 sts for the left sleeve, place m, 1 Rg-st, place m, 21 sts for the 2nd half of the back.

Break the working yarn in White.

SHAPING THE BACK NECKLINE WITH SHORT ROWS

This part is worked in Lilac and markers are slipped as you encounter them. Remove the BOR marker in the back.

Row 1: K21, M1R from the bar between sts (twisted), 1 Rg-st, M1R from the bar between sts (twisted), k12, M1R from the bar between sts (twisted), 1 Rg-st, M1R from the bar between sts (twisted), k1, turn work.

Row 2: Double st, p1, p1 (Rg-st), p14, p1 (Rg-st), p43, M1L from the bar between sts (twisted), p1 (Rg-st), M1L from the bar between sts (twisted), p12, M1L from the bar between sts (twisted), p1 (Rg-st), M1L from the bar between sts (twisted), p1, turn work.

Row 3: Double st, k1, k1 (Rg-st), k14, k1 (Rg-st), k44, M1R from the bar between sts (twisted), 1 Rg-st, M1R from the bar between sts (twisted), k14, M1R from the bar between sts (twisted), k1 (Rg-st), M1R from the bar between sts (twisted), k4, turn work.

Row 4: Double st, p4, p1 (Rg-st), p16, p1 (Rg-st), p45, M1L from the bar between sts (twisted), 1 Rg-st, M1L from the bar between sts (twisted), p14, M1L from the bar between sts (twisted), p1 (Rg-st), M1L from the bar between sts (twisted), p4, turn work.

Row 5: Double st, k4, k1 (Rg-st), k16, k1 (Rg-st), k46, k1 (Rg-st), k16, 1 Rg-st [= 128 sts].

In this spot, place a marker in a different color to mark the new BOR here at the raglan line on the right front.

RAGLAN LINES AND BEGINNING OF MAIN PATTERN

Follow Chart 1. Raglan line increases are always worked in the appropriate color of the pattern; after the Rg-sts, the pattern repeat is read from left to right; before the Rg-sts, the pattern repeat is read from right to left.

Row 1: Inc 1 = st #4 of the pattern repeat, work sts #5+6 of the pattern repeat once, work the pattern repeat (6 sts in width) 7 times widthwise, work sts #1+2 of the pattern repeat once, inc 1 = st #3 of the pattern repeat, 1 Rg-st, inc 1 = st #4 of the pattern repeat, work sts #5+6 of the pattern repeat once, work the pattern repeat (6 sts in width) 2 times widthwise, work sts #1+2 of the pattern repeat once, inc 1 = st #3 of the pattern repeat, 1 Rg-st, inc 1 = st #4 of the pattern repeat, work sts #5+6 of the pattern repeat once, work the pattern repeat (6 sts in width) 7 times widthwise, work sts #1+2 of the pattern repeat once, inc 1 = st #3 of the pattern repeat, 1 Rg-st, inc 1 = st #4 of the pattern repeat, work sts #5+6 of the pattern repeat once, work the pattern repeat (6 sts in width) 2 times widthwise, work sts #1+2 of the pattern repeat once, inc 1 = st #3 of the pattern repeat [= 136 sts].

Now, continue the pattern according to the chart and work raglan increases in every other round another 35 (41/47/53) times for front and back, and 29 (35/41/47) times for the sleeves. As a result, after all raglan increases, you now have 3 sts in White each before as well as after the Rg-sts = 120 (132/144/156) sts each for the front and back, and 78 (90/102/114) sts for each sleeve [= 400 (448/496/544) sts].

DIVIDING THE SLEEVES FROM THE BODY

Continuing to work in Main Pattern, work 120 (132/144/156) sts (front), while knitting the last st together with the following Rg-st working skp, transfer the 78 (90/102/114) sts for the left sleeve to a piece of waste yarn or spare cord for holding (note the row of the pattern repeat worked last), cast on 6 new underarm sts with 2 strands of working yarn held together, knit the next Rg-st together with the 1st st of the back working k2tog, work the remaining 119 (131/143/155) sts of the back, knitting the last st together with the following Rg-st working skp, transfer the 78 (90/102/114) sts for the right sleeve to a piece of waste

yarn or spare cord for holding, cast on 6 new underarm sts with 2 strands of working yarn held together (placing a marker for the new BOR after the 3rd stitch), knit the last Rg-st together with the next st of the front working k2tog [= 252 (276/300/324) sts].

Continue to work in the round in Main Pattern until the whole color sequence has been worked.

Then, work the flower motif according to Chart 2 once. To adjust the st count for the motif, during Rnd 1, either increase or decrease the number of sts listed for your size as follows, evenly spaced: +4 (-4/+4/-4) sts [= 256 (272/304/320)] sts.

HEM RIBBING

After having completed all rows of Chart 2, work Hem Ribbing Pattern *k1 in White, k1 in Lilac* continuously for 18 rounds. Break both strands of working yarn.

Now, work applied I-cord edging in Pink (see illustrated tutorial in Basics chapter on pages 24–25).

SLEEVES

Take up the formerly held 78 (90/102/114) sleeve sts with a short circular knitting needle or a double-pointed needle set and pick up and knit 6 sts in Lilac from the armhole edge of the body [= 84 (96/108/120) sts].

The sleeves are worked in the round.

Now, continue the Main Pattern, and work the round to the beginning of the underarm sts. These 6 underarm sts are worked in White, and to the right of (before) and to the left of (after) these sts, sleeve tapering decreases are worked as follows:

After the underarm sts, k2tog, work to last 2 sts before the underarm sts, skp, work 6 underarm sts.

Rep these decreases as follows: *in every other round, once, and in every 4th round, once*, rep from * to * a total of 11 times (22 decreases and 66 rounds).

Then, rep sleeve tapering decreases in every other round 2 times more = 26 decreases in all [= 58 (64/76/88) sts].

In the next round, decrease 6 sts evenly spaced.

Then work 2 in/5 cm in Ribbing Pattern [= 52 (58/70/82)] sts.

Now, work applied I-cord edging in Lilac.

COLLAR

Carefully dissolve the sts of the provisional crochet cast-on one by one and place the freed sts on the needle.

Now, work applied I-cord edging in Pink.

FINISHING

Carefully weave in all ends. Spread the sweater flat on an even surface, pull it into shape, cover it with wet cloths, and let it dry.

CHART 1

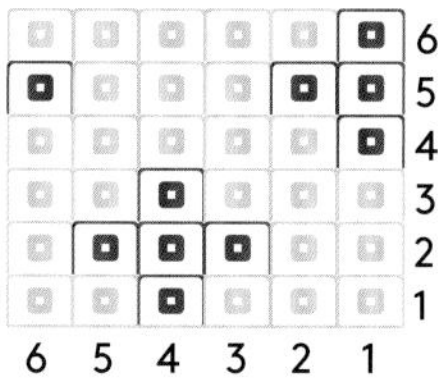

CHART 2

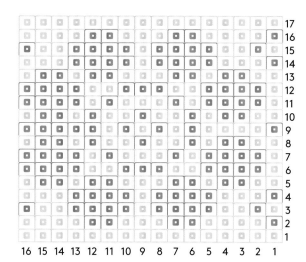

BONNIE
Cropped shirt with circular yoke

SIZES

S (M/L/XL)

Chest Circumference

37.7 (38.6/42.5/46.5) in/88 (98/108/118) cm

Total Length

17 in/43 cm

MATERIALS

- Jamieson & Smith Shetland Heritage; light fingering weight; 100% Real Shetland Wool; 120 yd/110 m per 0.9 oz/25 g skein

   Brown: 2 (2/3/3) skeins

   Vanilla Yellow: 4 (6/6/7) skeins

   Pure White: 2 (2/3/3) skeins

   Golden Yellow: 1 (1/2/2) skein/s

- US size 8 (5.0 mm) circular knitting needles in different lengths
- Extra cord or waste yarn for holding sleeve stitches
- Stitch markers
- Tapestry needle
- Scissors

GAUGE

In pattern: 18 sts and 24 rows = 4 x 4 in/10 x 10 cm

STITCH PATTERNS

Main Pattern

Stockinette stitch in charted colorwork pattern in the indicated order of work.

Neck Band/Collar Pattern

In rounds: *K1, p1*, rep from * to * continuously.

Mock Cable Pattern

Rnd 1: *Sl1, k1, yo, k1, pass the slipped st over the last 3 sts, p2*, rep from * to * continuously.

Rnds 2–3: *K3, p2*, rep from * to * continuously.

INSTRUCTIONS

The shirt is worked with 2 strands of yarn in the indicated colors held together.

Using US 8 (5.0 mm) needles and 1 strand each in Golden Yellow and Pure White held together, cast on 84 (90/96/96) sts, join work into the round, place a marker to indicate the BOR, and work 5 rnds in Neckband/Collar Pattern. The BOR is located at the end of the left sleeve/beginning of the front.

Work 2 rnds in stockinette stitch in Vanilla Yellow, while during the 1st round increasing after every other st by working M1R from the bar between sts (twisted) [= 126 (135/144/144) sts].

Then, continue according to the Chart; for Size M, in Rnd 4, increase 3 sts evenly spaced to adjust the stitch count to fit the pattern, placing a stitch marker on each of these sts. These 3 sts will be decreased again in the same spots in Rnd 7.

Rnd 12: *Work 3 sts, then M1R from the bar between sts (twisted), rep from * around [= 168 (180/192/192) sts].

Rnd 25: *Work 4 sts, then M1R from the bar between sts (twisted), rep from * around [= 210 (225/240/240) sts].

Rnd 39: *Work 5 sts, then M1R from the bar between sts (twisted), rep from * around [= 252 (270/288/288) sts].

Rnd 45: Increase sts evenly distributed as stated for the size worked:

Size M:

Increase 7 sts.

Size L:

Increase 12 sts.

Size XL:

*Work 6 sts, then M1R from the bar between sts (twisted), rep from * around [= 252 (277/300/336] sts].

All rnds of the chart have been completed at this point; continue in Vanilla Yellow in Mock Cable pattern:

Rnd 1: *K3, p2*, rep from * to * 50 (54/57/67) times, at the same time, either increasing (+) or decreasing (-) sts evenly distributed to adjust the stitch count to fit the pattern as stated for the size worked: -2 (-2/0/+4) sts [= 250 (275/300/340) sts].

Rnd 2: *Sl1, k1, yo, k1, pass the slipped sts over the last 3 sts, p2*, rep from * to * continuously.

Rnds 3–4: *K3, p2*, rep from * to * continuously.

Rep the last 3 rnds 3 times more.

DIVIDING THE SLEEVES FROM THE BODY

Continue as follows in Mock Cable pattern: work 80 (90/100/110) sts (back), transfer the next 45 (50/50/60) sts (right sleeve) to a piece of waste yarn or spare cord for holding, cast on 5 new underarm sts, work the next 80 (90/100/110) sts (front), transfer the next 45 (50/50/60) sts (left sleeve) to a piece of waste yarn or spare cord for holding, cast on 5 new underarm sts, place a marker to indicate the BOR.

Work the 3 rnds of the Mock Cable pattern 10 times in all (30 rnds), then bind off all sts knitwise.

SLEEVES

Take up the held 45 (50/50/60) sleeve sts again and place them on the needle, then pick up and knit 5 sts from the armhole edge at the side of the body, then bind off all sts knitwise. Rep for 2nd sleeve.

FINISHING

Carefully weave in all ends. Wash the shirt according to the manufacturer's washing instructions on the ball band of the yarn, spread it out on an even horizontal surface, and let it dry.

CHART

The charted pattern repeat is worked a total of 3 times + 3 rows heightwise.

HAILEY
Casual raglan sweater

◆◆◆

SIZES

S (M/L/XL/XXL)

Chest Circumference

39.5 (43.25/47.25/51.25/55) in/100 (110/120/130/140) cm

Length from Underarm

9 in/23 cm

Total Length

20.75 in/53 cm

MATERIALS

- Lang Yarns Yak; worsted weight; 70% pure new wool, 30% yak; 131 yd/120 m per 1.75 oz/50 g skein

  Sand 00949: 7 (8/9/10/11) skeins

  Stone Brown 0039: 3 (4/5/5/5) skeins

- US size 7 (4.5 mm) and US 8 (5.0 mm) circular knitting needles in different lengths

- Extra cord or waste yarn for holding sleeve stitches

- Stitch markers

- Tapestry needle

- Scissors

GAUGE

In stockinette stitch on US 7 (4.5 mm) needles: 18 sts and 26 rows = 4 x 4 in/10 x 10 cm

In pattern on US 8 (5.0 mm) needles: 22 sts and 20 rows = 4 x 4 in/10 x 10 cm

STITCH PATTERNS

Main Pattern

Stockinette stitch in charted colorwork pattern in the indicated order of work.

Ribbing Pattern

Alternate "k2, p2."

Raglan Stitches

2 sts in stockinette stitch.

Increases

Please refer to illustrated tutorial in Basics chapter on pages 17–18.

Short Rows

Please refer to illustrated tutorial in Basics chapter on page 21.

INSTRUCTIONS

Using US 7 (4.5 mm) needles and color Sand, cast on 96 sts and join work into the round, taking care not to twist the cast-on row. Place a marker to indicate the BOR = at the end of the front, before the Rg-sts, at the beginning of the left sleeve.

RAGLAN

Rnd 1: Slip marker, k2 (Rg-sts), place m, inc 1, k8 for the left sleeve, inc 1, place m, k2 (Rg-sts), place m, inc 1, k36 for the back, inc 1, place m, k2 (Rg-sts), place m, inc 1, k8 for the right sleeve, inc 1, place m, k2 (Rg-sts), place m, inc 1, k36 for the front, inc 1 [= 104 sts].

In subsequent rounds, slip markers as you encounter them.

Rnd 2: K2 (Rg-sts), k10 for the left sleeve, k2 (Rg-sts), k38 for the back, k2 (Rg-sts), k10 for the right sleeve, k2 (Rg-sts), k38 for the front.

Rep these 2 rnds another 23 (27/31/35/39) times, continuing the Raglan increases as described [= 288 (320/352/384/416) sts].

DIVIDING THE SLEEVES FROM THE BODY

K1 (Rg-st). Transfer the following sts to a piece of waste yarn or spare cord for holding: 1 Rg-st, the next 56 (64/72/80/88) sleeve sts as well as the next Rg-st, cast on 4 (5/6/7/8) new underarm sts, 1 Rg-st, knit the next 84 (92/100/108/116) sts (back) and the following Rg-st; transfer the next Rg-st as well as the following 56 (64/72/80/88) sleeve sts and the next Rg-st to a piece of waste yarn or spare cord for holding, cast on 4 (5/6/7/8) new underarm sts (placing a new marker in the middle of the sts to indicate the BOR), 1 Rg-st, knit the next 84 (92/100/108/116) sts (front) [= 180 (198/216/234/252) sts].

BODY

Knit 2 rnds in Sand.

Knit 2 rnds in Stone Brown, at the same time, during the 2nd rnd, inc +4 (+2/0/+6/+4) sts evenly spaced [= 184 (200/216/240/256) sts].

Change to US 8 (5.0 mm) needles, and in the next rnd, begin working from the Chart: work the pattern repeat (8 sts in width) 23 (25/27/30/32) times widthwise.

Work a total of 32 rnds in pattern = work the pattern repeat 4 times heightwise.

Break the working yarn in Sand.

Knit 2 rnds in Stone Brown, at the same time, during the last rnd, decrease 12 sts evenly spaced [= 172 (188/204/228/244) sts].

Then, work a total of 24 rnds in Ribbing Pattern: *k2, p2*, rep from * to * 43 (47/51/57/61) times.

After this, bind off all sts in pattern.

SLEEVES

Take up the formerly held 58 (66/74/82/90) sleeve sts (including the Rg-sts) again, and place them onto a US 7 (4.5 mm) circular knitting needle, pick up and knit 4 (5/6/7/8) underarm sts from the armhole edge at the side of the body, placing a marker to indicate the BOR after half of the sts [= 62 (71/80/89/98) sts].

Knit 2 rnds in Sand.

Knit 2 rnds in Stone Brown, at the same time, during the 2nd rnd, either increasing or decreasing +2 (+1/0/-1/-2) st(s) evenly spaced [= 64 (72/80/88/96) sts].

Change to US 8 (5.0 mm) needles, and in the next rnd begin working from the chart: work the pattern repeat (8 sts in width) 8 (9/10/11/12) times widthwise.

Work a total of 24 rnds in pattern = work the pattern repeat 3 times heightwise.

Break the working yarn in Sand.

Knit 2 rnds in Stone Brown, at the same time, during the 2nd rnd, decreasing 8 sts evenly spaced [= 56 (64/72/80/88) sts].

Then, work a total of 9 rnds in Ribbing Pattern: *k2, p2*, rep from * to * 14 (16/18/20/22) times.

In the next rnd, knit sts together as follows: *k2tog, p2*, rep from * to * 14 (16/18/20/22) times [= 42 (48/54/60/66) sts].

Now, work 9 rnds more as: *k1, p1*, rep from * to end of rnd.

Bind off all sts in pattern.

COLLAR

Using working yarn in Stone Brown, pick up and knit 104 sts from the cast-on edge at a rate of 1 st picked up from every st = 104 sts, beginning between the 2 Rg-sts at the end of the back and placing a marker to indicate the BOR.

Rnd 1: Skp, k8, k2tog, skp, k36, k2tog, skp, k8, k2tog, skp, k36, k2tog [= 96 sts].

Rnd 2: Knit all sts.

Rnd 3: Skp, k6, k2tog, skp, k34, k2tog, skp, k6, k2tog, skp, k34, k2tog [= 88 sts].

SHORT ROWS FOR SHAPING THE COLLAR

K9, turn work.

Double st, p55, turn work.

Double st, k57, turn work.

Double st, p59, turn work, k91 = the round ends at the front between the Rg-sts.

Work 16 rnds in the following stripe sequence:

1 st in Sand, 1 st in Stone Brown, rep from * to * 40 times.

Knit 1 rnd in Stone Brown.

Now, work 5 rnds more in Ribbing Pattern: *k2, p2*, rep from * to * 20 times, then bind off all sts in pattern.

Fold the collar to the inside of the garment and sew it to the cast-on edge.

FINISHING

Carefully weave in all ends. Wash the sweater according to the manufacturer's washing instructions on the ball band of the yarn, spread it out on an even horizontal surface, and let it dry.

CHART

CAITRIONA
Pullover with bat sleeves

◆◆◆

SIZES

S (M/L/XL/XXL)

Chest Circumference

37.75 (41/43.25/45.75/48) in/96 (104/110/116/122) cm [the batwing shape results in approx. 8.7 (9.9/11.0/13.0/13.8) in/22 (25/28/32/35) cm incorporated positive ease]

Raglan Line Length

18.9 in/48 cm

Length from Underarm

11 in/28 cm

Total Length

22.5 in/57 cm

MATERIALS

- Rauma Finull PT2; fingering/light sport weight; 100% Norwegian wool; 191 yd/175 m per 1.75 oz/50 g skein

  Lobster 4069: 3 (4/5/6/7) skeins

  White 0401: 3 (4/5/6/7) skeins

- Rauma Plum; lace weight; 70% super kid mohair, 30% polyamide/nylon; 274 yd/250 m per 0.9 oz/25 g skein

  Lobster 189: 3 (3/4/5/5) skeins

  White 003: 3 (3/4/5/5) skeins

- US size 7 (4.5 mm) circular knitting needles in different lengths
- Stitch markers
- Tapestry needle
- Scissors

GAUGE

In pattern: 24/25 sts and 24 rows = 4 x 4 in/10 x 10 cm

STITCH PATTERNS

Main Pattern

Stockinette stitch in charted colorwork pattern in the indicated order of work.

Ribbing Pattern

K1-tbl, p1, rep from * to * continuously.

Short Rows

Please refer to illustrated tutorial in Basics chapter on page 21.

Increases

Please refer to illustrated tutorial in Basics chapter on pages 17–18.

Raglan Stitch

Work 1 st in Lobster.

INSTRUCTIONS

Always work with 1 strand of Finull PT2 held together with 1 strand of Plum in the same color.

SHAPING THE BACK NECKLINE

Cast on 88 (104/120/136/152) sts in White. Join work into the round, taking care not to twist the cast-on row, and place a marker to indicate the BOR = at the end of the front before the Rg-st.

Row 1 in White: K1 (Rg-st), place m, inc 1, k24 (28/32/36/40) for the left sleeve, inc 1, k1 (Rg-st), place m, inc 1, k16 (20/24/28/32) for the back, inc 1, place m, k1 (Rg-st), place m, inc 1, k24 (28/32/36/40) for the right sleeve, inc 1, place m, k1 for the front, turn work. In subsequent rounds, slip markers as you encounter them.

Row 2 in White: Double st, p1 (Rg-st), work 26 (30/34/38/42) sts (right sleeve), p1 (Rg-st), work 18 (22/26/39/34) sts (back), p1 (Rg-st), work 26 (30/34/38/42) sts (left sleeve), p1 (Rg-st), p1 (front), turn work.

Row 3 in White: Double st, k1 (Rg-st), place m, inc 1, k26 (30/34/38/42) (left sleeve), inc 1, k1 (Rg-st), place m, inc 1, k18 (22/26/30/34) for the back, inc 1, place m, k1 (Rg-st), place m, inc 1, k26 (30/34/38/42) (right sleeve), inc 1, place m, k1, and k1 (front), turn work.

Row 4: Double st, p1, p1 (Rg-st), p28 (32/36/40/44) (right sleeve), p1 (Rg-st), p20 (24/28/32/36) (back), p1 (Rg-st), p28 (32/36/40/44) (left sleeve), p1 (Rg-st), p1, and p1 (front), turn work.

BEGINNING OF COLORWORK PATTERN AND RAGLAN INCREASES

Rnd 1: Double st, k1, 1 Rg-st in Lobster.

LEFT SLEEVE

Size S:

Inc 1 (st #5 of the pattern repeat), work sts #6–8 of the pattern repeat once, work the pattern repeat 3 times widthwise, work sts #1–3 of the pattern repeat once, inc 1 (st #4 of the pattern repeat) [= 32 sts]

Size M:

Inc 1 (st #7 of the pattern repeat), work st #8 of the pattern repeat once, work the pattern repeat 4 times widthwise, work st #1 of the pattern repeat once, inc 1 (st #2 of the pattern repeat) [= 36 sts].

Size L:

Inc 1 (st #5 of the pattern repeat), work sts #6–8 of the pattern repeat once, work the pattern repeat 4 times widthwise, work sts #1–3 of the pattern repeat once, inc 1 (st #4 of the pattern repeat) [= 40 sts].

Size XL:

Inc 1 (st #7 of the pattern repeat), work st #1 of the pattern repeat once, work the pattern repeat 5 times widthwise, work st #1 of the pattern repeat once, inc 1 (st #2 of the pattern repeat) [= 44 sts].

Size XXL:

Inc 1 (st #5 of the pattern repeat), work sts #6–8 of the pattern repeat once, work the pattern repeat 5 times widthwise, work sts #1–3 of the pattern repeat once, inc 1 (st #4 of the pattern repeat) [= 48 sts].

All sizes:

1 Rg-st in Lobster.

BACK

Size S:

Inc 1 (st #5 of the pattern repeat), work sts #6–8 of the pattern repeat once, work the pattern repeat 2 times widthwise, work sts #1–3 of the pattern repeat once, inc 1 (st #4 of the pattern repeat) [= 24 sts].

Size M:

Inc 1 (st #7 of the pattern repeat), work st #8 of the pattern repeat once, work the pattern repeat 3 times widthwise, work st #1 of the pattern repeat once, inc 1 (st #2 of the pattern repeat) [= 28 sts].

Size L:

Inc 1 (st #5 of the pattern repeat), work sts #6–8 of the pattern repeat once, work the pattern repeat 3 times widthwise, work sts #1–3 of the pattern repeat once, inc 1 (st #4 of the pattern repeat) [= 32 sts].

Size XL:

Inc 1 (st #7 of the pattern repeat), work st #8 of the pattern repeat once, work the pattern repeat 4 times widthwise, work st #1 of the pattern repeat once, inc 1 (st #2 of the pattern repeat) [= 36 sts].

Size XXL:

Inc 1 (st #5 of the pattern repeat), work sts #6–8 of the pattern repeat once, work the pattern repeat 4 times widthwise, work sts #1–3 of the pattern repeat once, inc 1 (st #4 of the pattern repeat) [= 40 sts].

All sizes:

1 Rg-st in Lobster.

RIGHT SLEEVE

See left sleeve, 1 Rg-st in Lobster.

FRONT

Work as for the back = 8 increases in all in each round [= 116 (132/148/164/180) sts].

Rnd 2: 1 Rg-st, 32 (36/40/44/48) sts in pattern for left sleeve, 1 Rg-st, 24 (28/32/36/40) sts in pattern for back, 1 Rg-st, 32 (36/40/44/48) sts in pattern for right sleeve, 1 Rg-st, 24 (28/32/36/40) sts in pattern for front.

Now, continue according to the Chart, repeating the pattern repeat continuously widthwise and 12 times heightwise, at the same time, in every other round, increasing 8 sts for raglan shaping, 47 times in all [= 492 (508/524/540/556) sts].

DIVIDING BODY AND SLEEVES

Remove marker, work 1 Rg-st, transfer 126 (130/134/138/142) sts (left sleeve) to a piece of waste yarn or spare cord for holding, cast on 4 (6/8/10/12)

new underarm sts with both strands held together, work 1 Rg-st, work 118 (122/126/134/138) sts (back) in pattern, work 1 Rg-st in Lobster, transfer 126 (130/134/138/142) sts (right sleeve) to a piece of waste yarn or spare cord for holding, cast on 4 (6/8/8/12) new underarm sts with both strands held together, work 1 Rg-st in Lobster, work 118 (122/126/134/138) sts (front) in pattern, place a new BOR marker in this spot [= 248 (260/272/292/304) sts].

For Sizes S/L/XXL, the Rg-sts as well as the 1st and last of the underarm sts are incorporated into the colorwork pattern, yielding a full pattern repeat each before and after the underarm sts.

For Sizes M and XL, the Rg-sts are reallocated to the underarm sts and worked in one color (Lobster).

Work the underarm sts all in Lobster.

Work a total of 28 rnds (work the pattern repeat 2.5 times heightwise) from the armhole.

Break the working yarn in White, and continue in Lobster:

Knit the underarm sts, place m, within the back, decrease 19 (15/15/15/15) sts evenly spaced, place m, knit the following underarm sts, place m, within the

front, decrease 19 (15/15/15/15) sts evenly spaced, place m.

Knit the underarm sts as before, work the sts of the back in Ribbing Pattern, beginning and ending with "p1," knit the following underarm sts, work the sts of the front in Ribbing Pattern, beginning and ending with "p1."

After having worked a total of 15 rnds, bind off all sts knitwise.

SLEEVES

Take up the formerly held 126 (130/134/138/142) sleeve sts again and place them on the needle. Pick up and knit 4 (6/8/8/12) underarm sts from the armhole edge at the side of the body (placing a new marker in the middle of the sts to indicate the BOR), and continue in Main Pattern according to the Chart. The newly cast-on underarm sts are worked in one color (Lobster) throughout [= 130 (136/142/146/154) sts].

For sleeve tapering, in every rnd, decrease 1 st each before and after the underarm sts as follows:

Work 1 (2/3/3/5) underarm stitch(es), knit the last underarm st together with the 1st st of the colorwork pattern by working skp (the underarm st in Lobster is located on top), work the sts of the round to the last st in Main Pattern before the underarm sts. Knit this st together with the 1st underarm st working k2tog (the underarm st in Lobster is located on top), work 1 (2/3/3/5) underarm stitch(es).

Rep these decreases 38 times more = 78 decreases [= 52 (58/64/68/76) sts].

Break the working yarn in White and continue in Lobster.

Knit 2 (3/4/4/6) underarm sts, within the following 48 (52/56/60/64) sts, decrease 5 (7/9/11/13) sts evenly spaced, knit 2 (3/4/4/6) underarm sts.

Knit 2 (3/4/4/6) underarm sts, *p1, k1-tbl*, rep from * to * 21 (22/23/24/25) times, p1, knit 2 (3/4/4/6) underarm sts.

After having completed 15 rnds, bind off all sts knitwise.

NECKBAND

Pick up and knit 72 (88/104/120/136) sts in Lobster from the cast-on edge, place a marker to indicate the BOR, and work 8 rnds in stockinette stitch. Then, purl 1 rnd = fold line.

Work an additional 8 rnds in stockinette stitch, then bind off all sts.

Fold the neckband to the inside of the garment and sew it to the cast-on edge.

FINISHING

Carefully weave in all ends. Wash the sweater according to the manufacturer's washing instructions on the ball band of the yarn, and let it dry spread out flat on an even horizontal surface.

CHART

SHONA
Casual oversized vest

SIZES

One size

Chest Circumference

51.25 in/130 cm

Total Length

29.5 in/75 cm

MATERIALS

- Rosy Green Wool Big Merino Hug; medium/worsted weight; 100% organic Merino wool extra fine; 175 yd/160 m per 3.5 oz/100g

  Cream 118: 4 skeins

  Caramel 136. 2 skeins

  Amethyst 134: 1 skein

- Five 1 in/26 mm buttons (buttons shown in sample are Agoya mother-of-pearl buttons by Jim Knopf)

- US size 9 (5.5 mm) circular knitting needles in different lengths

- Stitch holders or two pieces of waste yarn for holding shoulder stitches

- Stitch markers

- Tapestry needle

- Scissors

GAUGE

In stockinette stitch: 16/17 sts and 25 rows = 4 x 4 in/10 x 10 cm

In pattern: 18 sts and 25 rows = 4 x 4 in/10 x 10 cm

STITCH PATTERNS

Main Pattern

Stockinette stitch in charted colorwork pattern in the indicated order of work.

CONSTRUCTION NOTES

The vest starts at the neckline and is worked from the wide shoulder seam outward. Fronts and back are shaped by increases to the right and left of the shoulder seam. The wide collar Is knitted onto the main part afterwards; the buttonhole band is knitted at the same time as the main part.

INSTRUCTIONS

Using US 9 (5.5 mm) needles and Cream, cast on 48 sts.

Row 1: K1 (selv st), k1, place m, work 4 shoulder sts as "p1, k2, p1," place m, k36 (back), place m, work 4 shoulder sts as "p1, k2, p1," place m, k1, k1 (selv st).

Row 2: P1 (selv st), pfb, work 4 shoulder sts as "k1, p2, k1," pfb, p34 (back), pfb, work 4 shoulder sts as "k1, p2, k1," pfb, p1 (selv st) [= 52 sts].

Row 3: K1 (selv st), k1, kfb, 4 shoulder sts in established pattern, kfb, k36, kfb, 4 shoulder sts in established pattern, kfb, k1, k1 (selv st) [= 56 sts].

Row 4: P1 (selv st), p2, pfb, 4 shoulder sts in established pattern, kfb, p38, kfb, 4 shoulder sts in established pattern, kfb, p2, p1 (selv st) [= 60 sts].

Rep Rows 3–4 another 7 times (14 rows) [= 116 sts].

NECKLINE SHAPING ON THE FRONTS

Row 1: Beginning at the left front, k1 (selv st), M1R from the bar between sts, k17, kfb, 4 shoulder sts in established pattern, kfb, k68, kfb, 4 shoulder sts in established pattern, kfb, k17, M1R from the bar between sts, k1 (selv st) [= 122 sts].

Row 2: P1 (selv st), p19, kfb, 4 shoulder sts in established pattern, kfb, p70, kfb, 4 shoulder sts in established pattern, kfb, p19, selv st [= 126 sts].

Row 3: K1 (selv st), k20, kfb, 4 shoulder sts in established pattern, kfb, k72, kfb, 4 shoulder sts in established pattern, kfb, k20, k1 (selv st) [= 130 sts].

Row 4: P1 (selv st), p21, pfb, 4 shoulder sts in established pattern, pfb, p74, pfb, 4 shoulder sts in established pattern, pfb, p21, p1 (selv st) [= 134 sts].

Row 5: K1 (selv st), M1R from the bar between sts, k22, kfb, 4 shoulder sts in established pattern, kfb, k76, kfb, 4 shoulder sts in established pattern, kfb, k22, M1R from the bar between sts, k1 (selv st) [= 140 sts].

Row 6: Work as Row 4 [= 144 sts].

Row 7: K1 (selv st), M1R from the bar between sts, k25, kfb, 4 shoulder sts in established pattern, kfb, k80, kfb, 4 shoulder sts in established pattern, kfb, k25, M1R from the bar between sts, k1 (selv st) [= 150 sts].

Row 8: Work as Row 4 [= 154 sts].

Row 9: Cast on 2 new sts (at the end of the previous row = Row 8), k29, kfb, 4 shoulder sts in established pattern, kfb, k84, kfb, 4 shoulder sts in established pattern, kfb, k29, cast on 2 new sts [= 162 sts].

Row 10: Work as Row 4 [= 166 sts].

Row 11: Cast on 3 new sts at the end of the previous row = Row 10, k33, kfb, 4 shoulder sts in established pattern, kfb, k88, kfb, 4 shoulder sts in established pattern, kfb, k33, cast on 3 new sts = 176 sts.

Row 12: Work as Row 4 [= 180 sts].

Row 13: Cast on 4 new sts (at the end of the previous row = Row 12), k38, kfb, 4 shoulder sts in established pattern, kfb, k92, kfb, 4 shoulder sts in established pattern, kfb, k38, cast on 4 new sts = 192 sts.

Row 14: Work as Row 4 [= 196 sts].

Row 15: Cast on 17 new sts (at the end of the previous row = Row 14), k44, kfb, 4 shoulder sts in established pattern, kfb, k96, kfb, 4 shoulder sts in established pattern, kfb, k44, cast on 17 new sts [= 234 sts].

The 17 new sts are: 6 sts for the front, 11 sts for the button band/buttonhole band.

Row 16: K1 (selv st), *p1, k1*, work from * to * 5 times total = button band, p51, kfb, 4 shoulder sts in established pattern, kfb, p98, kfb, 4 shoulder sts in established pattern, kfb, p51, *k1, p1*, work from * to * 5 times total, slip 1 with yarn in front of work (selv st) [= 238 sts].

Row 17: K1 (selv st), 10 sts button band, k52, kfb, 4 shoulder sts in established pattern, kfb, k100, kfb, 4 shoulder sts in established pattern, kfb, k52, 10 sts buttonhole band, slip 1 with yarn in front of work (selv st) [= 242 sts].

Row 18: K1 (selv st), 10 sts button band, p53, kfb, 4 shoulder sts in established pattern, kfb, p102, kfb, 4 shoulder sts in established pattern, kfb, p53, 10 sts buttonhole band, slip 1 with yarn in front of work (selv st) [= 246 sts].

Row 19: K1 (selv st), 10 sts button band, k54, kfb, 4 shoulder sts in established pattern, kfb, k104, kfb, 4 shoulder sts in established pattern, kfb, k54, 1st buttonhole: *p1, k1*, rep from * to * 2 times, bind off 3 sts without using the working yarn by passing 1 st over another, cast on 3 new sts, work the remaining 3 sts in established pattern, slip 1 with yarn in front of work (selv st) [= 250 sts].

Work 4 more buttonholes, spaced 22 rows from each other, the same way.

Row 20: K1 (selv st), 10 sts button band, p55, kfb, 4 shoulder sts in established pattern, kfb, p106, kfb, 4 shoulder sts in established pattern, kfb, p55, 10 sts buttonhole band, slip 1 with yarn in front of work (selv st) = 254 sts. **_At the same time,_** to adjust the stitch count for the stitch pattern, on each front, M1L twice, evenly spaced (twisted); on the back, M1L 5 times, evenly spaced (twisted) = 58 sts for each front/113 sts for the back [= 263 sts].

Shoulder increases have now been completed, and the fronts and the back are worked separately.

LEFT FRONT

Keep only the sts of the left front on the needle, transferring the 4 shoulder sts to a stitch holder or safety pin for holding, and transferring the sts of the back and the right front separately to a spare cord or piece of waste yarn for holding.

Now, work according to the Chart; the 10 sts of the button band as well as the selv st will be worked in Cream in the following 37 rows.

Work the selv st and 10 sts for the button band in Cream, work the pattern repeat (6 sts in width) 9 times widthwise, work sts #1–3 of the pattern repeat once, k1 in Cream (selv st).

Work the pattern repeat (16 rows in height) 2 times heightwise, then work only Rows 1–5 once heightwise.

Then, transfer all sts to a spare cord or piece of waste yarn for holding.

BACK

Take up the 113 sts of the back again, place them on the needle, and work according to the Chart:

Work the selv st in Cream, work the pattern repeat (6 sts in width) 18 times widthwise, work sts #1–3 of the pattern repeat once, work the selv st in Cream.

Work the pattern repeat (16 rows in height) 2 times heightwise, then work only Rows 1–5 once heightwise.

Then, transfer all sts to a spare cord or piece of waste yarn for holding.

RIGHT FRONT

Take up the 69 sts of the right front again, place them on the needle, and work mirror-inverted to the left front.

Work the pattern repeat (16 rows in height) 2 times heightwise, then work only Rows 1–5 once heightwise.

In Row 6 of the chart (WS), join all pieces as follows:

Work 69 sts (right front), 113 sts (back), 69 sts (left front) [= 251 sts].

Then, work wide stripes in the following color sequence: Selv st, 10 sts button band, 229 sts stockinette stitch, 10 sts buttonhole band, selv st.

10 rows in Cream.

12 rows in Caramel.

12 rows in Amethyst.

Work 12 rows in Cream, in Row 11, decrease 4 sts, evenly spaced, but not placing any decreases within the button band/buttonhole band [= 247 sts].

Then, work Rows 9–12 of the Chart 2 times heightwise = 8 rows as follows:

Selv st, 10 sts button band in Cream, work the pattern repeat (6 sts in width) 37 times widthwise, work sts #1–3 of the pattern repeat once, 10 sts buttonhole band, work 1 st in Cream (selv st).

Work 4 rows in Cream as follows:

Selv st, 10 sts button band, 225 sts stockinette stitch, 10 sts buttonhole band, selv st.

Work 8 rows in the following color sequence:

RS rows: Selv st, 10 sts button band band in Cream, *k1 in Caramel, k1 in Cream*, rep from * to * 112 times, k1 in Caramel, 10 sts buttonhole band, work the selv st in Cream.

WS rows: Work all sts and colors as they appear.

Work 1 RS row in Cream, then bind off all sts on the WS knitwise.

COLLAR

The collar is worked in garter stitch.

On the WS of the fabric, pick up and knit 105 sts in Caramel along the cast-on edge = 35 sts along each front and 35 sts along the back).

Row 1: Slip the selv st knitwise, k34, place m, p3, place m, k29, place m, p3, place m, k34, knit the selv st.

Row 2: Slip the selv st knitwise, k4, yo, k30, yo, k3, yo, k29, yo, k3, yo, k30, yo, k5 [= 111 sts].

Row 3: Slip the selv st knitwise, k4, knit the yo, k30, knit the yo, p3, knit the yo, k29, knit the yo, p3, knit the yo, k30, knit the yo, k5.

Rep Rows 2–3 another 14 times (30 rows total) [= 195 sts].

In the next row, bind off all sts loosely knitwise.

ARMHOLE FINISHING

Left sleeve: Beginning at the underarm, pick up and knit 35 sts along the front, take up the formerly held 4 sts, place them on the needle and work the sts as they appear, pick up and knit 34 sts along the back [= 73 sts]. Join to work in the round.

Rnds 1–6: *K1, p1*, rep from * to * 17 times, k1, p1, k2, p1, *k1, p1, rep from * to * 17 times.

Then, bind off all sts loosely in pattern.

Work the right sleeve mirror-inverted.

FINISHING

Carefully weave in all ends. Wash the vest according to the manufacturer's washing instructions on the ball band of the yarn, spread it out on an even horizontal surface, and let it dry. Sew on the buttons, right side facing out.

CHART

The charted pattern repeat is repeated widthwise and heightwise as often as stated in the instructions.

ENYA
V-neck sweater with fluffy balloon sleeves

◆◆◆

SIZES

S (M/L/XL/XXL)

Chest Circumference

33.5 (37.5/41.25/45.25/49.25) in/85 (95/105/115/125) cm

Total Length

21.7 in/55 cm

Length from Underarm

17.0 in/43 cm

MATERIALS

- Rauma Finull; fingering/light sport weight; 100% Norwegian wool; 191 yd/175 m per 1.75 oz/50 g skein)

  Moss 4129: 2 (2/3/3/4) skeins

  Pink 4138: 1 (1/2/2/2) skein/s

  White 0401: 2 (2/3/3/3) skeins

- Rauma Plum; lace weight; 70% super kid mohair, 30% polyamide/nylon; 274 yd/250 m per 0.9 oz/25 g per skein

  White 003: 3 (3/3/3/3) skeins

- US size 2.5 (3.0 mm), US 4 (3.5 mm), and US 11 (8.0 mm) circular knitting needles in different lengths

- Spare cord or waste yarn for holding sleeve stitches

- Stitch markers

- Scissors

- Tapestry needle

GAUGE

In pattern: 24 sts and 25 rows = 4 x 4 in/10 x 10 cm

STITCH PATTERNS

Main Pattern

Stockinette stitch in charted colorwork pattern in the indicated order of work.

Raglan Stitches

2 sts in stockinette stitch in White.

INSTRUCTIONS

Using US 4 (3.5 mm) needles and Moss, cast on 87 (91/103/107/119) sts and work in the following stitch sequence and according to the Chart:

If needed, place markers, and slip them when you encounter them in subsequent rows.

Row 1 (RS): *Left front:* k1 (selv st), 2 sts in White, **inc 1 in Moss**, place a marker to indicate the BOR, 2 Rg-sts in White, *left sleeve:* **inc 1 in Moss**, *2 sts in White, 2 sts in Moss*, rep from * to * 3 (3/4/4/5) times, 2 sts in White, **inc 1 in Moss**, 2 Rg-sts in White, *back:* **inc 1 in Moss**, *2 sts in White, 2 sts in Moss*, rep from * to * 11 (12/13/14/15) times, 2 sts in White, **inc 1 in Moss**, 2 Rg-sts in White, *right sleeve:* **inc 1 in Moss**, *2 sts in White, 2 sts in Moss*, rep from * to * 3 (3/4/4/5) times, 2 sts in White, **inc 1 in Moss**, 2 Rg-sts in White, *right front:* **inc 1 in Moss**, 2 sts in White + 1 st in Moss with both strands held together [= 95 (99/111/115/127) sts].

Row 2: Purl all sts, working all colors as they appear, at the end of the row, inc 1 in Moss with both strands of working yarn held together for the front [= 96 (100/112/116/128) sts].

Work the raglan increases (shown in bold font) another 23 (27/31/35/39) times, incorporating the increased sts into the pattern in the established manner.

For V-neck shaping, additionally inc 1 st 8 (8/8/10/11) times, 2 sts 2 (3/4/4/5) times, 3 sts twice, 4 sts once, and incorporate these increased sts into the charted pattern as well = 23 (25/27/29/31) sts for the V-neck for each half of the front. When having completed all increases, in the following row, join both fronts, hereby incorporating the selv sts of the right and left front into the pattern = 48 (52/56/60/64) sts for the front. From here on, work is continued in the round, and raglan increases are finished.

DIVIDING THE SLEEVES FROM THE BODY

Starting at the BOR on the left sleeve, before the Rg-sts, transfer the sts of the left sleeve to a piece of waste yarn or spare cord for holding as follows: 2 Rg-sts, 60 (64/72/76/84) sleeve sts, 2 Rg-sts. With both strands of working yarn held together, cast on 6 new underarm sts (placing a marker after half of the sts for the new BOR), then work the 94 (106/118/130/142) sts of the back in pattern. Transfer the sts of the right sleeve to another piece of waste yarn or spare cord for holding as follows: 2 Rg-sts, 60 (64/72/76/84) sleeve sts, 2 Rg-sts. With both strands

of working yarn held together, cast on 6 new underarm sts, then work the 96 (108/120/132/144) sts of the front in pattern [= 202 (226/250/274/298) sts].

Continue the pattern to an overall height of 15.5 in/39 cm measured from the cast-on edge on the back, working the pattern repeat (10 rows in height) 10 times heightwise.

Then, work an additional 5 in/13 cm in the following color sequence:

1 st in Pink, 1 st in Moss, rep from * to * continuously.

RUFFLED EDGE

Rnd 1: Using US 2.5 (3.0 mm) needles and Moss, rep *k1, yo* to end of round [= 404 (452/500/548/596) sts].

Rnd 2: Knit all sts and yarn overs.

Rnds 3–4: Knit all sts.

Bind off all sts knitwise.

NECK BAND

Pick up sts for the neckband from the cast-on edge and neckline edge as follows, the BOR is located at the right Rg-st on the back: Using US 2.5 (3.0 mm) needles and Moss, pick up and knit 38 (42/46/50/54) sts along the back, 12 sts along the sleeve, 36 (40/44/48/52) sts along the left half of the front, 2 sts in the deepest point of the V-neck, 36 (40/44/48/52) sts along the right half of the front, 12 sts along the sleeve.

Rnd 1: *P2, k2*, rep from * to * continuously to 2 sts before the 2 center sts in the deepest point of the V-neck, purl these 2 sts before the center sts, and knit the 2 center sts, *p2, k2*, rep from * to * to end of round.

Rnd 2: Work all sts, keeping in ribbing pattern, to 1 st before the 2 center sts: K2tog (the st before the 2 center sts and the 1st center st), then skp (the 2nd center st and the following st).

Rep Rnds 1 and 2 another 3 times. Work these decreases in every other round 3 times more, then bind off all sts loosely in pattern.

SLEEVES

The sleeves are worked with 2 strands of Plum held together.

Take up the formerly held 64 (68/76/80/88) sleeve sts again and place them on a US 4 (3.5 mm) needle, and, with 2 strands of Plum held together, pick up and knit 6 underarm sts from the armhole edge at the side of the body [= 70 (74/82/86/94) sts].

Then, change to US 11 (8.0 mm) needles and work 16 in/41 cm in stockinette stitch in the round.

Change to US 4 (3.5 mm) needles and work 3 rnds in stockinette stitch.

In the next rnd, *k1, skp*, rep from * to *.

Work 1 rnd in stockinette stitch, then bind off all sts knitwise.

FINISHING

Carefully weave in all ends. Wash the sweater according to the manufacturer's washing instructions on the ball band of the yarn and let it dry spread out flat on an even horizontal surface.

CHART

The charted pattern repeat is repeated widthwise and heightwise as often as stated in the instructions.

SHARNI
Sweater with a poncho look

◆◆◇

SIZES

S (M/L/XL)

Chest Circumference

39.5 (43.25/47.25/51.25) in/100 (110/120/130) cm
(includes positive ease of + 4 in/10 cm)

Length from Underarm

Approx. 4.75 in/12 cm (adjustable)

Total Length

Approx. 22.5 in/57 cm (including collar)

MATERIALS

- ◆ Pascuali Alpaca Fino; DK/light worsted; 100% alpaca; 131 yd/120 m per 1.75 oz/50 g

  Brown 034: 5 (6/7/8) skeins

  Yellow 032: 5 (6/7/8)

  Brick Red 035: 1 (1/1/1) skein

- ◆ US size 6 (4.0 mm) and US 7 (4.5 mm) circular knitting needles in different lengths

- ◆ US size 6 (4.0 mm) double-pointed needle set for sleeves, if desired

- ◆ Stitch markers

- ◆ Tapestry needle

- ◆ Scissors

GAUGE

In pattern on US 7 (4.5 mm) needles: 24 sts and 25 rows = 4 x 4 in/10 x 10 cm

STITCH PATTERNS

Main Pattern

Stockinette stitch in charted colorwork pattern in the indicated order of work.

Ribbing Pattern

In rounds: Alternate "k2, p2."

INSTRUCTIONS

Using US 7 (4.5 mm) needles, cast on 108 (112/116/120) sts in Brown. Join work into the round, taking care not to twist the cast-on row; place a marker to indicate the BOR (center of the back).

Work according to the following pattern sequence:

Work 2 rnds in Brown, at the same time, during the 2nd rnd, after every other st, M1R from the bar between sts (twisted) [= 162 (168/174/180) sts].

Work 4 rnds in colorwork pattern from Chart 1.

Work 2 rnds in Yellow, at the same time, during the 2nd rnd, adjust the stitch count to fit the pattern as listed for your size: -2 (+2/-4/0) [= 160 (170/170/180) sts].

Work 7 rnds in colorwork pattern from Chart 2.

Work 2 rnds in Yellow, at the same time, during the 2nd rnd, adjusting the stitch count to fit the pattern as listed for your size: 0 (-2/-2/0) sts [= 160 (168/168/180) sts].

Work 6 rnds in colorwork pattern from Chart 3.

Work 2 rnds in Yellow, at the same time, during the 2nd rnd, adjusting the stitch count to fit the pattern as listed for your size: +2 (0/+4/0) sts [= 162 (168/174/180) sts].

Work 1 rnd in Brown.

Work 2 rnds in Yellow, at the same time, during the 2nd rnd, after every 3rd st, M1R from the bar between sts (twisted) [= 216 (224/232/240) sts].

Work 17 rnds in colorwork pattern from Chart 4.

Work 2 rnds in Yellow, at the same time, during the 2nd rnd, after every 4th st, M1R from the bar between sts (twisted) [= 270 (280/290/300) sts].

Work 1 rnd in Brown, at the same time, increasing to adjust the stitch count to fit the pattern as listed for your size: +2 (0/+2/0) [= 272 (280/292/300) sts].

Work 7 rnds in colorwork pattern from Chart 5.

Work 2 rnds in Yellow, at the same time, during the 1st rnd, decreasing to adjust the stitch count to fit the pattern as listed for your size: -2 (0/-2/0) [= 270 (280/290/300) sts].

Work 1 rnd in Brown.

Work 1 rnd in Yellow, at the same time, increasing from the bar between sts (twisted) as listed for your size:

Size S:

After every 9th st, M1R from the bar between sts (twisted) [= 300 sts].

Sizes M, L, XL:

After every 5th st, M1R from the bar between sts (twisted) [= 336/348/360 sts].

Work 4 rnds in colorwork pattern from Chart 1.

Work 2 rnds in Yellow, at the same time, during the 2nd rnd, adjusting the stitch count to fit the pattern as listed for your size: +4 (0/+4/0) sts [= 304 (336/352/360) sts].

Work 7 rnds in colorwork pattern from Chart 6, at the same time, during the 6th rnd, decreasing to adjust the stitch count to fit the pattern as listed for your size: -4 (0/-4/0) sts [= 300 (336/348/360) sts].

Work 1 rnd in Yellow, at the same time increasing by working M1R from the bar between sts (twisted) as listed for your size:

Size M:

Increase after every 42nd st, 8 times around [= 344 sts].

Size L:

Increase after every 13th st, 12 times, and after every 12th st, 16 times [= 376 sts].

Size XL:

Increase after every 6th st, 18 times, and after every 7th st, 36 times [= 414 sts].

Work 6 rnds in colorwork pattern from Chart 3, at the same time, for size XL only, during the 6th rnd, increasing 2 sts to adjust the stitch count to fit the pattern [= 416 sts].

Work 2 rnds in Yellow, at the same time, for size XL only, during the 1st round, decreasing 2 sts [= 414 sts].

Work 1 rnd in Brown.

DIVIDING THE SLEEVES FROM THE BODY

Work 2 rnds in Yellow, at the same time, during the 2nd rnd, dividing the sleeve sts from the body as follows:

Starting at the BOR in the center back:

Work 55 (62/66/71) sts (right half of back), transfer 40 (48/56/64) sleeve sts to a spare cord or piece of waste yarn for holding, cast on 2 new underarm sts, work 110 (124/132/143) sts (front), transfer 40 (48/56/64) sleeve sts to a spare cord or piece of waste yarn for holding, cast on 2 new underarm sts, work the remaining 55 (62/66/72) sts (left half of the back) [= 224 (252/268/290) sts].

Break both strands of working yarn. Slip all sts of the right half of the back up to the newly cast-on underarm sts below the right sleeve, to the right needle without working them.

Place a new marker for the BOR in the middle of the underarm sts.

Work 17 rnds in colorwork pattern from Chart 7, at the same time, during the 1st round, adjusting the stitch count to fit the pattern as listed for your size: +4 (0/ -4/-2) sts [= 228 (252/264/288) sts].

Work 2 rnds in Yellow, at the same time, during the 1st rnd, adjusting the stitch count to fit the pattern as listed for your size: -4 (0/+4/0) sts [= 224 (252/270/288) sts].

Work 1 rnd in Brown.

Work 2 rnds in Yellow.

Work 7 rnds in colorwork pattern from Chart 5.

Work 2 rnds in Yellow.

Work 1 rnd in Brown.

Work 2 rnds in Yellow, at the same time, during the 2nd rnd, decreasing 24 (24/22/24) sts, evenly spaced, by working skp [= 200 (228/248/264) sts].

Change to US 6 (4.0 mm) needles and work 8 rnds in Ribbing Pattern, then bind off all sts in pattern.

SLEEVES

Using either a circular needle for Magic Loop or a dou-ble-pointed needle set in size US 6 (4.0 mm), take up the formerly held 40 (48/56/64) sleeve sts again, pick up and knit 2 sts from the underarm sts at the side of the body, and join into the round.

Work 20 rnds in Ribbing Pattern, working "k2 in Yellow, p2 in Brown," then break the working yarn.

Work 2 rnds in Brick Red in Ribbing Pattern, then bind off all sts in pattern.

NECKBAND

Using US 6 (4.0 mm) needles and Brown, pick up and knit 112 (116/120/124) sts from the cast-on edge, and work 6 rnds in Ribbing Pattern.

In the next round, decrease by knitting every pair of knit sts together using k2tog while continuing to purl each of the purl sts.

Work an additional 5 rnds in *p2, k1* ribbing, then bind off all sts in pattern.

FINISHING

Carefully weave in all ends. Wash the sweater accord-ing to the manufacturer's washing instructions on the ball band of the yarn, and let it dry spread out flat on an even horizontal surface.

CHART 1

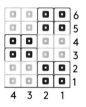

CHART 2

CHART 3

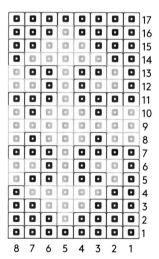

CHART 4

CHART 5

CHART 6

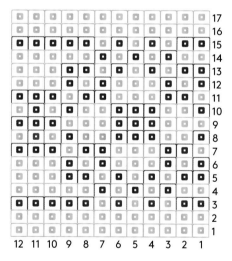

CHART 7

Work in the sequence listed in the instructions.

BRIANNA
Sweater with wide raglan stripes

◆◆◆

SIZES

S (M/L/XL/XXL)

Chest Circumference

37.75 (38.5/41.25/45/48.5) in/88 (98/105/114/123) cm

Length from Underarm

Approx. 9.9 in/25 cm

Total Length

Approx. 22 in/56 cm

MATERIALS

- Rosy Green Wool Cheeky Merino Joy; sport weight; 100% organic Merino wool extra fine; 350 yd/320 m per 3.5 oz/100 g skein

  Orange 102: 3 (3/4/4/5) skeins

  Alpine White 65: 2 (2/3/3/3) skeins

- US size 2.5 (3.0 mm) and US 4 (3.5 mm) circular knitting needles in different lengths

- US size 2.5 (3.0 mm) and US 4 (3.5 mm) double-pointed needle sets for sleeves, if desired

- Stitch markers

- Tapestry needle

- Scissors

GAUGE

In pattern on US 4 (3.5 mm) needles: 28 sts and 29/30 rows = 4 x 4 in/10 x 10 cm

STITCH PATTERNS

Main Pattern

Stockinette stitch in charted colorwork pattern in the indicated order of work.

Garter Stitch in the Round (Sleeve Cuff and Hemline)

Alternate "knit 1 rnd, purl 1 rnd."

Raglan Stitches

Over a width of 23 sts: *k1 in Orange, k1 in White*, work from * to * a total of 11 times, k1 in Orange.

Neckband Ribbing

Alternate "k1, p1".

INSTRUCTIONS

Using US 4 (3.5 mm) needles and color White, cast on 152 sts and join work into the round, taking care not to twist the cast-on row.

Work 1 rnd in White, while at the same time, dividing the sts as follows:

The BOR is located after the Rg-sts at left at the end of the Front.

Place m, work 21 sts (left sleeve), place m, 23 sts (Rg-sts), place m, 9 sts (back), place m, 23 sts (Rg-sts), 21 sts (right sleeve), place m, 23 sts (Rg-sts), 9 sts (front), 23 sts (Rg-sts).

Now, begin working the pattern according to the Chart:

In subsequent rounds, slip markers as you encounter them.

Left sleeve: Inc 1 in White, work the pattern repeat (6 sts in width) 3 times widthwise, work sts #1–3 of the pattern repeat once, inc 1 in White, 23 Rg-sts.

Back: Inc 1 in White, work 1 full pattern repeat (6 sts in width) widthwise, work sts #1–3 of the pattern repeat once, inc 1 in White, 23 Rg-sts.

Right sleeve: Inc 1 in White, work the pattern repeat (6 sts in width) 3 times widthwise, work sts #1–3 of the pattern repeat once, inc 1 in White, 23 Rg-sts.

Front: Inc 1 in White, work 1 full pattern repeat (6 sts in width) widthwise, work sts #1–3 of the pattern repeat once, inc 1 in White, 23 Rg-sts.

In the next round (= Rnd 2 of the chart), work all sts according to the pattern as established = 160 sts.

Rep Raglan increases as described above 32 (38/44/50/56) times more, incorporating the increased sts into the pattern in the established manner [= 416 (464/512/560/608) sts].

DIVIDING THE SLEEVES FROM THE BODY

From this point on, the Main Pattern is worked over the 23 former Rg-sts, too.

Transfer the 87 (99/111/123/135) sts of the left sleeve to a piece of waste yarn or spare cord for holding, cast on 11 new underarm sts, work the 112 (124/136/148/160) sts of the back in Main Pattern according to the Chart, transfer the next 87 (99/111/123/135) sts of the right sleeve to a piece of waste yarn or spare cord for holding, cast on 11 new underarm sts, work the 112 (124/136/148/160) sts of the front in Main Pattern according to the Chart, place

a marker to indicate the BOR [= 246 (270/294/318/342) sts].

Incorporate the underarm sts into the colorwork pattern in the established manner.

Then, continue in Main Pattern to a height of approx. 20.5 in/52 cm (measured in the center of the back from the cast-on edge).

Now, work 10 rounds in Orange in garter stitch, at the same time, during the 1st round, decreasing 24 sts, evenly spaced, by working skp, then bind off all sts knitwise.

SLEEVES

Take up the 87 (99/111/123/135) sleeve sts again, place them on the needle, and pick up and knit 12 underarm sts from the armhole edge at the side of the body, pick up and knit 1 additional st at the corner.

Incorporate the underarm sts into the colorwork pattern and work an additional 5.5 in/14 cm. The last round should be a Rnd 6 of the chart [= 99 (111/123/135/147) sts].

Now, change to US 2.5 (3.0 mm) needles and work for 4 in/10 cm (30 rounds) in the following pattern: *k1 in Orange, k1 in White*, rep from * to * continuously. At the same time, during the 1st rnd, decrease 1 st by working skp once [= 98 (110/122/134/146) sts].

Work an additional 18 rnds in Orange in garter stitch, while at the same time, during the 1st round, decreasing 26 sts evenly spaced [= 72 (84/96/108/120) sts].

Bind off all sts knitwise.

NECK BAND

The BOR is located before the Rg-sts on the back:

Using US 6 (4.0 mm) double-pointed needles and Orange, pick up and knit sts from the cast-on edge at a rate of 1 st picked up from every st.

Place m, **k1**, place m, 55 sts (back) in *k1, p1* Ribbing Pattern, rep from * to * 27 times, k1, place m, **k1**, place m, work 21 sts (sleeve) as *k1, p1*, rep from * to * 10 times, k1, place m, **k1**, place m, 55 sts (front) in *k1, p1* Ribbing, rep from * to * 27 times, k1, place m, **k1**, place m, work 21 sts (sleeve) as *k1, p1*, rep from * to * 10 times, do not work the last st.

In the next round, k3tog each st in bold with the st before and after it as described below, replacing the marker before and after the remaining st:

Next round: Insert the tip of the right needle from left to right (knitwise) into the last st of the previous round and the next knit st together and slip to right needle, then insert it from left to right (knitwise) into the 1st st of the Back and slip to right needle—there are now 3 sts on the right needle, the center st on top—knit these 3 sts together (decrease), work 53 sts (back), decrease as described, work 19 sts (left sleeve), decrease as described, work 53 sts (front), decrease as described, work 19 sts (right sleeve).

Rep these decreases in every other round 2 times more.

Then, bind off all sts in pattern.

FINISHING

Carefully weave in all ends. Wash the sweater according to the manufacturer's washing instructions on the ball band of the yarn and let it dry spread out flat on an even horizontal surface.

CHART

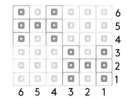

The charted pattern repeat is repeated widthwise and heightwise as often as stated in the instructions.

GEILLIS
Colorful dress with circular yoke

SIZES

S (M/L/XL)

Chest Circumference

37 (41/45/48.75) in/94 (104/114/124) cm

Total Length

Approx. 33.5 in/85 cm

MATERIALS

- Holst Garn Supersoft; light fingering weight; 100% wool; 314 yd/287 m per 1.75 oz/50 g skein

  Red 077: 3 (3/4/4) skeins

  Rose 014: 1 (1/2/2) skein/s

  Yellow 088: 1 (1/2/2) skein/s

  Pink 015: 2 (2/2/2) skeins

  Orange 075: 1 (1/1/1) skein

  Bleached White 049: 1 (1/1/1) skein

  Green 067: 1 (1/1/1) skein

  Magenta 018: 1 (1/1/1) skein
- US size 2.5 (3.0 mm) and US 4 (3.5 mm) circular knitting needles in different lengths
- US size 4 (3.5 mm) double-pointed needle set for sleeves, if desired
- US E-4 (3.5 mm) crochet hook
- Stitch markers
- Tapestry needle
- Scissors

GAUGE

In pattern on US 4 (3.5 mm) needles: 28 sts and 30 rows = 4 x 4 in/10 x 10 cm

STITCH PATTERNS

Main Pattern

Stockinette stitch in charted colorwork pattern in the indicated order of work.

Ribbing Pattern

In rounds: Alternate "k1, p1."

Crochet Bobble

Insert the crochet hook into the indicated loop of the stitch, pull the working yarn through to form a loop, *yarn over hook, insert the crochet hook into the same insertion point again, and pull the working yarn through*, rep from * to * 3 times more. Pull the working yarn through all loops on the hook, yarn over hook once more, and pull the working yarn through the individual loop on the hook. Now, insert the crochet hook from back to front into the st below the current stitch, pull the working yarn through the st and through both loops on the hook and tighten. Place the st onto the right tip of the knitting needle.

Short Rows

Please refer to illustrated tutorial in Basics chapter on page 21.

INSTRUCTIONS

Using US 4 (3.5 mm) needles and Red, cast on 130 (134/138/142) sts and join into the round, taking care not to twist the cast-on row. Place m at the BOR located in the center of the back.

Work 2 rnds in reverse stockinette stitch.

Work 4 rnds as *k1 in Yellow, k1 in Red*, rep from * to * continuously.

Work 2 rnds in Yellow in stockinette stitch.

In Red, work short rows for neckline shaping:

Row 1: K37 (39/41/43), turn work.

Row 2: Double stitch, p75 (77/79/81), turn work.

Row 3: Double stitch, k77 (79/81/83), turn work.

Row 4: Double stitch, p79 (81/83/85), turn work.

Row 5: Double stitch, k80 (82/84/86), turn work.

Row 6: Double stitch, p81 (83/85/87), turn work.

Knit to end of rnd.

In the next rnd, after every other stitch, M1R from the bar between sts (twisted) [= 195 (201/207/213) sts].

Work 5 rnds in colorwork pattern from Chart 1, while adjusting the stitch count to fit the pattern, during the 1st round, increasing as follows: +5 (+4/+3/+2) [= 200 (205/210/215) sts].

Work 6 rnds in colorwork pattern from Chart 2, while adjusting the stitch count to fit the pattern, for Sizes M and XL only, during the 1st round, increasing 1 st.

Work 1 rnd in Yellow, while adjusting the stitch count to fit the pattern, decreasing as follows: -5 (-5/-3/-3) [= 195 (201/207/213) sts].

Work 1 rnd in Green, at the same time, after every 3rd stitch, M1R from the bar between sts (twisted) [= 260 (268/276/284) sts].

Work 7 rnds in colorwork pattern from Chart 3.

Work 1 rnd in Green.

Work 1 rnd in Pink.

Work 1 rnd in Green, at the same time, after every 4th stitch, M1R from the bar between sts (twisted) [= 325 (335/345/355) sts].

Work 1 rnd in Pink, while adjusting the stitch count to fit the pattern, increasing as follows: +2 (+1/0/+2) sts [= 327 (336/345/357) sts].

Work 5 rnds in colorwork pattern from Chart 4.

Work 1 rnd in Pink.

Work 1 rnd in Green.

Work 1 rnd in Orange.

Work 1 rnd in Green, while adjusting the stitch count to fit the pattern, increasing as follows: +3 (+4/+5/+5) [= 330 (340/350/360) sts].

Work 5 rnds in colorwork pattern from Chart 5.

Work 1 rnd in Pink, while adjusting the stitch count to fit the pattern, decreasing 5 sts evenly spaced [= 325 (335/345/355) sts].

Work 1 rnd in Orange.

Work 1 rnd in Magenta, at the same time, after every 5th stitch, M1R from the bar between sts (twisted) [= 390 (402/414/426) sts].

Work 11 rnds in colorwork pattern from Chart 6, while adjusting the stitch count to fit the pattern during the 1st round as listed for your size: 0 (-2/-4/+4) [= 390 (400/410/430) sts].

Work 1 rnd in Magenta, while adjusting the stitch count to fit the pattern, increasing or decreasing as listed for your size: 0 (+2/+4/-4) [= 390 (402/414/426) sts].

Work 1 rnd in Orange, at the same time increasing by working M1R from the bar between sts (twisted) as listed for your size:

Size S:

After every 9th stitch, 30 times in all, after every 10th stitch, 12 times in all.

Size M/L/XL:

After every 6th stitch, M1R from the bar between sts (twisted)

[= 432 (469/483/497) sts].

Work 1 rnd in Rose, while adjusting the stitch count to fit the pattern, increasing or decreasing as listed for your size: -2 (+1/-3/+3) sts [= 430 (470/480/500) sts].

Work 7 rnds in colorwork pattern from Chart 7.

Work 1 rnd in Rose.

Work 3 rnds in colorwork pattern from Chart 8.

Work 1 rnd in Rose.

Work 1 rnd in Red.

Work 6 rnds in colorwork pattern from Chart 9, while adjusting the stitch count to fit the pattern during the 1st round as listed for your size: +2 (-2/0/-2) [= 432 (468/480/498) sts].

Work 1 rnd in Red, at the same time increasing by working M1R from the bar between sts (twisted) as listed for your size:

Size L:

After every 13th stitch, 16 times in all, and after every 17th stitch, 16 times in all.

Size XL:

After every 10th stitch, 39 times in all, and after every 9th stitch, 12 times in all, M1R from the bar between sts (twisted).

[= 432 (468/512/548) sts].

Work 1 rnd in Yellow.

Work 7 rnds in colorwork pattern from Chart 10.

Work 1 rnd in Red.

Work 6 rnds in colorwork pattern from Chart 2.

Work 1 rnd in Yellow.

DIVIDING THE SLEEVES FROM THE BODY

Work 1 round in Yellow, as follows:

Work 66 (73/80/87) sts (1st half of the back), transfer 84 (89/96/100) sts (right sleeve) to a spare cord or piece of waste yarn for holding, cast on 6 new underarm sts (placing a marker for the new BOR after half of the sts), work 132 (145/160/174) sts (front), transfer 84 (89/96/100) sts (left sleeve) to a spare cord or piece of waste yarn for holding, cast on 6 new underarm sts, work 66 (73/80/87) sts (2nd half of the back) [= 276 (303/332/360) sts].

Break the working yarn, slip all sts up to the new BOR to the right needle without working them.

Work 1 rnd in Green, while adjusting the stitch count to fit the pattern for Size M only by increasing 1 st [= 304 sts].

Work 7 rnds in colorwork pattern from Chart 3.

* Work 1 rnd in Green, work 1 rnd in Pink *, rep from * to * 2 times, while adjusting the stitch count to fit the pattern during the last round as listed for your size: 0 (-1/+1/0) [= 276 (303/333/360) sts].

Work 5 rnds in colorwork pattern from Chart 4.

Work 1 rnd in Pink.

Work 1 rnd in Green.

Work 1 rnd in Orange.

Work 1 rnd in Green, while adjusting the stitch count to fit the pattern as listed for your size: +4 (-3/-3/0) [= 280 (300/330/360) sts].

Work 5 rnds in colorwork pattern from Chart 5.

Work 1 rnd in Pink.

Work 1 rnd in Orange.

Work 1 rnd in Magenta.

Work 11 rnds in colorwork pattern from Chart 6.

Work 1 rnd in Magenta.

Work 1 rnd in Orange.

Work 1 rnd in Rose.

Work 7 rnds in colorwork pattern from Chart 7.

Work 1 rnd in Rose.

Work 3 rnds in colorwork pattern from Chart 8.

Work 1 rnd in Rose.

Work 1 rnd in Red, while adjusting the stitch count to fit the pattern for Size S only: decrease 4 sts evenly spaced [= 276 sts].

Work 6 rnds in colorwork pattern from Chart 9.

Work 1 rnd in Red.

Work 1 rnd in Yellow, while adjusting the stitch count to fit the pattern for Size L only: decrease 2 sts evenly spaced [= 328 sts].

Work 7 rnds in colorwork pattern from Chart 10.

Work 1 rnd in Yellow.

Work 1 rnd in Red.

Work 6 rnds in colorwork pattern from Chart 2.

Work 1 rnd in Yellow.

Work 1 rnd in Green.

Work 7 rnds in colorwork pattern from Chart 3.

Work 1 rnd in Green.

Work 1 rnd in Pink.

Work 1 rnd in Green.

Work 1 rnd in Pink, while adjusting the stitch count to fit the pattern for Size L only: increase 2 sts evenly spaced [= 330 sts].

Work 5 rnds in colorwork pattern from Chart 4.

Work 1 rnd in Pink.

Work 1 rnd in Green.

Work 1 rnd in Orange.

Work 1 rnd in Green, while adjusting the stitch count to fit the pattern for Size S only: increase 4 sts evenly spaced [= 280 sts].

Work 5 rnds in colorwork pattern from Chart 5.

Work 1 rnd in Pink.

Work 1 rnd in Orange.

Work 1 rnd in Magenta.

Work 11 rnds in colorwork pattern from Chart 6.

Work 1 rnd in Magenta.

Work 1 rnd in Orange.

Work 1 rnd in Rose.

Work 7 rnds in colorwork pattern from Chart 7.

Work 1 rnd in Rose.

Work 3 rnds in colorwork pattern from Chart 8.

Work 1 rnd in Rose, while knitting together every 9th and 10th st by working skp = -28 (-30/-33/-36) sts [= 252 (270/297/324) sts].

Then, change to US size 2.5 (3.0 mm) needles and Red, and work 4.75 in/12 cm in Ribbing Pattern, while adjusting the stitch count to fit the pattern for Size L only during the 1st rnd: decrease 1 st, then bind off all sts in pattern.

SLEEVES

Take up the formerly held 84 (89/96/100) sleeve sts and place them on the needle, then pick up and knit 6 underarm sts in Yellow from the armhole edge at the side of the body (placing a marker after half of the sts to indicate the BOR) [= 90 (95/102/106) sts].

Work 1 rnd in Yellow in stockinette stitch, while decreasing 26 (25/26/26) sts evenly spaced [= 64/70/76/80 sts].

Work 3 rnds in Ribbing Pattern, then bind off all sts in pattern.

FINISHING

Carefully weave in all ends. Wash the dress according to the manufacturer's washing instructions on the ball band of the yarn, spread it out on an even horizontal surface, and let it dry.

CHART 1

For Chart 1 only, work ▣ as Crochet Bobble.

CHART 2

CHART 3

CHART 4

CHART 5

CHART 6

CHART 7

CHART 8

CHART 9

CHART 10

KIRSTIE
Cool sweater with buttons

SIZES

S (M/L/XL)

Chest Circumference

45 (48.75/52.75/56.75) in/114 (124/134/144) cm
(includes positive ease of + 8 in/20 cm)

Length from Underarm

Approx. 12.5 in/32 cm

Total Length

Approx. 20.5 in/52 cm

MATERIALS

- Pascuali Tibetan; medium/worsted weight; 70% virgin wool, 30% yak; 137 yd/125 m per 1.75 oz/50 g skein

  Off White 100: 5 (6/7/8) skeins

  Orange 117: 4 (5/6/7) skeins

  Brown 111: 2 (3/4/5) skeins

- Three approx. 1 in/26 mm buttons (buttons shown in sample are coconut buttons in wood pattern by Jim Knopf)
- US size 6 (4.0 mm) and US 7 (4.5 mm) circular knitting needles in different lengths
- US size 7 (4.5 mm) double-pointed needle set for sleeves
- Stitch markers
- Tapestry needle
- Scissors

GAUGE

In pattern on US 7 (4.5 mm) needles: 19 sts and 27 rows = 4 x 4 in/10 x 10 cm

STITCH PATTERNS

Main Pattern

Stockinette stitch in charted colorwork pattern in the indicated order of work.

Ribbing Pattern

Alternate *k2 in either Orange or Brown, p2 in White*.

INSTRUCTIONS

Using US 7 (4.5 mm) needles and Off White, cast on 46 sts.

Row 1 (RS): K1 (selv st), kfb, place m, k2, place m, kfb, k36, kfb, place m, k2, place m, kfb, k1 (selv st) [= 50 sts].

In subsequent rounds, slip markers as you encounter them.

Row 2 (WS): P1 (selv st), p1, pfb, p2, pfb, p38, pfb, p2, pfb, p1, p1 (selv st) [= 54 sts].

Rep Rows 1 and 2 another 8 times [= 118 sts].

Now, in addition to shoulder increases, increases for the front neckline are being worked as follows:

At the beginning as well as at the end of each row, cast on additional sts as follows: 1 st once, then in every 4th row 1 st twice, 2 sts once, in every other row 2 sts once, 3 sts once, 5 sts once [= 228 sts].

Increases for the 2 halves of the front are finished at this point; just the increases to the right and left of the shoulders will be continued in every row, 3 (7/11/15) times more, 240 (256/272/288) sts = 120 (128/136/144) sts for the back, 58 (62/66/70) sts for each of the 2 fronts, plus 2 sts for each shoulder.

The back and the front are now continued separately to the height of the armhole:

RIGHT HALF OF THE FRONT

Work 34 (40/28/26) rows in stockinette stitch, cast on 8 additional sts at the neckline edge, transfer the sts to a spare cord or piece of waste yarn for holding. (The last row worked is a RS row.)

LEFT HALF OF THE FRONT

Work 34 (40/28/26) rows in stockinette stitch, in the next WS row, incorporate the sts of the right half into the current row and purl them.

For Sizes S/M, transfer the sts to a spare cord or piece of waste yarn for holding now, for Sizes L/XL, work an additional 18/26 rows in stockinette stitch, then transfer the sts to a spare cord or piece of waste yarn for holding.

BACK

Work 34 (40/46/52) rows in stockinette stitch, then incorporate the sts of the front into the current row, join into the round, and work 1 round, at the same time, either at the right or left underarm, place a marker to indicate the new BOR [= 248 (264/280/296) sts].

Work 1 rnd in Off White, while adjusting the stitch count to fit the pattern, increasing or decreasing as listed for your size: +2 (-4/0/+4) sts [= 250 (260/280/300) sts].

Now, work 20 rnds in the charted colorwork pattern.

Then, work 25 rnds in Orange in stockinette stitch, while adjusting the stitch count to fit the pattern for Size S only, during the last rnd decreasing 2 sts.

Work an additional 20 rnds in Ribbing Pattern: *k2 in Orange, p2 in White*, rep from * to * continuously. Bind off all sts in pattern.

SLEEVES

Pick up and knit 58 (70/82/94) sts in Off White around the armhole edge and place a marker to indicate the BOR at the underarm.

Work 1 rnd in Off White, adjusting the stitch count to fit the pattern, increasing or decreasing as listed for your size: +2 (0/-2/-4) sts [= 60 (70/80/90) sts].

Work 20 rnds in the charted colorwork pattern but using Brown instead of Orange.

Then, work 40 rnds in Brown in stockinette stitch, during the last round adjusting the stitch count to fit the pattern, decreasing as listed for your size: 0 (-2/0/-2) sts.

Work an additional 20 rnds in Ribbing Pattern: *k2 in Brown, p2 in White*, rep from * to * continuously. Bind off all sts in pattern.

NECKLINE, BUTTON PLACKET, AND BUTTONHOLE PLACKET

Using Off White, pick up and knit 39 sts along the vertical section of the neckline on the left front.

Work 1 WS row as follows: p1 (selv st), p1, *k2, p2* 9 times, p1 (selv st).

Work 11 rows more in the previously established stitch sequence, then bind off the sts with a narrow applied I-cord, casting on only 1 additional st (see instructions in Basics chapter on pages 24–25).

In the buttonhole placket on the right half of the front, 3 buttonholes will be worked. For this part, proceed as follows: Slip 2 sts purlwise, *pass the st to the right over the st to the left, slip the next st purlwise*, rep from * to * 2 times more. Return the last st remaining after binding off to the left needle, then cast on 3 new sts. In the next row, work these sts in pattern.

Pick up and distribute sts for the right placket the same way as on the left front.

In Row 6, work 3 buttonholes as instructed above, as follows: P1 (selv st), p1, k2, buttonhole, 12 sts in established pattern, buttonhole, 12 sts in established pattern, buttonhole, p1, p1 (selv st).

Finish the buttonhole placket the same way as on the left front.

Now, place the buttonhole placket (right part) on top of the button placket (left part), and sew both into the opening at the front of the garment using mattress stitch (see instructions in Basics chapter on page 26).

NECKLINE RIBBING

Using Brown, pick up and knit 142 sts along the neckline edge, beginning at the right front (51 sts along the front, 40 sts along the back, 51 sts along the front).

Work 1 WS row as follows: Slip sts #1+2 with yarn in front of work, slightly tightening the working yarn at the same time (for the I-cord), *p2, k2*, rep from * to * 34 times, p4.

Work 1 RS row as follows: Slip sts #1+2 with yarn in back of work, slightly tightening the working yarn, work in established pattern to end of row.

Work 4 more rows in Brown.

Next RS row: Slip 2, *p2 in White, k2 in Brown*, rep from * to * 24 times, p2 in White, k2 in Brown.

Work a total of 4 rows, then bind off all sts in pattern.

FINISHING

Carefully weave in all ends. Sew the buttons to the neckline placket. Wash the sweater according to the manufacturer's washing instructions on the ball band of the yarn and let it dry spread out flat on an even horizontal surface.

CHART

The charted pattern repeat is repeated widthwise and heightwise as often as stated in the instructions. In the body, the colors are worked as shown; in the sleeves, Brown is used instead of Orange.

BRIDGET
Poncho

◆◆◆

SIZES

One size

Bottom Width

51.25 in/130 cm

Total Length

20 in/50 cm

MATERIALS

- Ístex Lettlopi; medium/worsted weight; 100% pure new wool; 109 yd/100 m per 1.75 oz/50 g skein

  Gray 0054: 3 skeins

  Blue 1403: 5 skeins

- Two 1 in/28 mm buttons (sample in pictures shows 4-hole mother-of-pearl buttons by Jim Knopf in Matte Blue)

- US size 8 (5.0 mm) circular knitting needles in different lengths

- Stitch markers

- Tapestry needle

- Scissors

GAUGE

In pattern: 20 sts and 36 rows = 4 x 4 in/10 x 10 cm

STITCH PATTERNS

Main Pattern

Stockinette stitch in charted colorwork pattern in the indicated order of work.

Ribbing Pattern

In rounds: Alternate "k2, p2."

Collar Ribbing

In RS rows: Alternate "k1, p1"; in WS rows, work all sts as they appear (knitting the knits and purling the purls).

Center Stitch Increase (ctr-st inc)

Increases are worked alternatingly in Blue and Gray, creating a vertical stripe pattern: Work as instructed to the center st, insert the right needle from back to front into the right leg of the st below the center st, and knit this st through the back loop (twisted). Then, knit the center st. Now, insert the left needle from back to front into the left leg of the st below the center st, and knit this st through the back loop (twisted).

INSTRUCTIONS

COLLAR

Cast on 91 sts in Blue and work 14 rows in Ribbing Pattern for the Collar: k1 (selv st), *k1, p1*. Rep from * to * 44 times, k1, slip 1 with yarn in front of work (selv st).

In Rows 5 and 11, at the end of the row, work a buttonhole each: 86 sts in established pattern, 1 buttonhole.

The buttonholes are worked as follows: Slip 2 sts purlwise, *pass the st to the right over the st to the left, slip the next st purlwise*, rep from * to * 2 times more. Return the last st remaining after binding off to the left needle, then cast on 3 new sts. In the next row, incorporate the increased sts into the pattern.

BODY

Work 1 rnd in Blue in stockinette stitch as follows: selv st, work 4 sts, within the next 81 sts, increase 34 sts evenly spaced, now join work into the round by knitting the last 5 sts of the row together with the 1st 5 sts in pairs, so the buttonhole placket on the right half of the collar is located on top of the button placket on the left half of the collar, placing a marker to indicate the BOR before the 4th pair of sts [= 120 sts].

Then, work according to Chart and divide the sts into sections as follows:

Rnd 1 of the Chart in Blue: 27 sts for the remainder of a full pattern repeat, place m, 1 center st, place m, 29 sts for another full pattern repeat, place m, 1 center st, place m, 29 sts for another full pattern repeat, place m, 1 center st, place m, 29 sts for another full pattern repeat, place m, 1 center st [= 120 sts].

In subsequent rounds, slip markers as you encounter them.

Rnd 2 of the Chart: Work the 29 sts of the pattern repeat, ctr-st inc in Gray, work the 29 sts of the pattern repeat, ctr-st inc in Gray, work the 29 sts of the pattern repeat, ctr-st inc in Gray, work the 29 sts of the pattern repeat, ctr-st inc in Gray [= 128 sts].

Rnd 3 of the Chart: Work the 29 sts of the pattern repeat, 1 st in Gray, 1 center st in Blue, 1 st in Gray, work the 29 sts of the pattern repeat, 1 st in Gray, 1 center st in Blue, 1 st in Gray, work the 29 sts of the pattern repeat, 1 st in Gray, 1 center st in Blue, 1 st in Gray, work the 29 sts of the pattern repeat, 1 st in Gray, 1 center st in Blue, 1 st in Gray.

Rnd 4 of the Chart: Work the 29 sts of the pattern repeat, 1 st in Gray, ctr-st inc in Blue, 1 st in Gray, work the 29 sts of the pattern repeat, 1 st in Gray, ctr-st inc in Blue, 1 st in Gray, work the 29 sts of the pattern repeat, 1 st in Gray, ctr-st inc in Blue, 1 st in Gray, work the 29 sts of the pattern repeat, 1 st in Gray, ctr-st inc in Blue, 1 st in Gray [= 136 sts].

Work the the charted pattern repeat (14 rounds in height) 5 times heightwise = 70 rnds, at the same time, in every other round, working ctr-st incs to the right of (before) and to the left of (after) the center st as described, 33 times in all [= 384 sts].

End with an even rnd without increases.

Now, continue in Ribbing Pattern as stated below. During the 1st rnd, increase 3 sts evenly spaced for each section.

Work the next 93 sts as follows: *p2, k2*, rep from * to *, while adjusting the stitch count to fit the pattern by increasing 3 sts, ending with p2 = 98 sts, 1 center st, work from ** to ** 4 times in all.

Work 14 more rnds in Ribbing Pattern without increases.

Then, bind off all sts loosely in pattern.

FINISHING

Carefully weave in all ends. Sew on the buttons. Wash the poncho according to the manufacturer's washing instructions on the ball band of the yarn and let it dry spread out flat on an even horizontal surface.

CHART

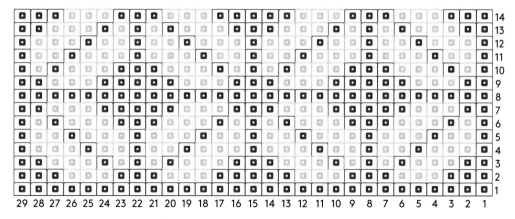

The charted pattern repeat is repeated widthwise and heightwise as often as stated in the instructions.

CLAIRE
Short jacket

◆◆◆

SIZES

S–M (L–XL)

Chest Circumference

37.8 (45.7) in/96 (116) cm

Length from Underarm

16.5 in/42 cm

Total Length

25.6 in/65 cm

MATERIALS

- ◆ Holst Garn Cielo; Aran weight; 42% alpaca, 42% Merino wool, 16% polyamide/nylon; 137 yd/125 m per 1.75 oz/50 g skeln

    Blue: 6 (7) skeins

    White: 6 (7) skeins

- ◆ US size 10 (6.0 mm) circular knitting needles in different lengths
- ◆ Stitch markers
- ◆ Tapestry needle
- ◆ Scissors

GAUGE

In pattern: 19 sts and 21 rows = 4 x 4 in/10 x 10 cm

STITCH PATTERNS

Main Pattern

Stockinette stitch in charted colorwork pattern in the indicated order of work.

Collar and Sleeve Cuff Pattern (Garter Stitch)

Garter stitch in turned rows: Knit all sts in RS and WS rows.

Garter stitch in the round:

Rnd 1 (RS): Knit all sts

Rnd 2 (WS): Purl all sts

Alternate these 2 rounds.

I-Cord

Please refer to illustrated tutorial in Basics chapter on pages 24–25.

CONSTRUCTION NOTES

Work starts with the small mandarin collar. Pick up sts for the shoulders and the back from the collar, then first the fronts and later the sleeves are shaped through increases. When all increases have been finished, the garment is worked from the top down until completion.

INSTRUCTIONS

MANDARIN COLLAR

Cast on 12 sts in White.

Row 1: Slip 3 sts knitwise with yarn in back of work, slightly tighten the working yarn (I-cord-edge), 6 sts in garter stitch, k3 (I-cord-edge).

Row 2: Slip 3 sts purlwise, with yarn in front of work, slightly tighten the working yarn (I-cord-edge), 6 sts in garter stitch, p3 (I-cord-edge).

Rep Rows 1 and 2 for a total of 66 rows.

Now, *knit sts #1+2 individually, knit sts #3+4 together left-leaning as ssk, return the 3 sts to the left needle* and rep the steps from * to * until only the 3 sts of the I-cord remain on the needles, then transfer these 3 sts to a stitch holder or piece of waste yarn for holding (a safety pin works well for this purpose).

Now, pick up and knit 12 sts along the cast-on edge of the collar, and work similarly in the opposite direction but for only 65 rows, then work I-cord on the wrong side of the fabric as follows:

Purl sts #1+2 individually, purl sts #3+4 together left-leaning as ssp. Return these 3 sts individually to the left needle and here, too, rep the steps from * to * until only the 3 sts of the I-cord remain on the needles. Transfer these 3 sts to a safety pin for holding.

KNITTING ON THE BACK AND SHOULDERS

Note: (Inc 1) = make 2 sts from 1 st (either knit in front and back or purl in front and back). If not in parentheses, work increase as instructed on pages 17–18.

Using Blue, pick up and knit 42 sts from the I-cord edge, counting from the center outward, 24 sts each remain at the sides in the garter stitch part.

WS: *Right front:* p1 (selv st), (inc 1), place m, *right shoulder:* p3, place m, *back:* (inc 1), p30, (inc 1), place m, *left shoulder*: p3, place m, *left front:* (inc 1), p1 (selv st) [= 46 sts].

RS: Begin charted pattern, as below.

Left front: work sts #9–12 of the pattern repeat from Chart 1, including increases: pick up and knit 1 additional st for the neckline from the I-cord of the collar, 1 st in pattern, (inc 1) [= 4 sts].

K3 in Blue for the shoulder.

Back: work the pattern repeat from Chart 1, including increases, 3 times widthwise: (inc 1), 32 sts in pattern, (inc 1) [= 36 sts].

K3 in Blue for the shoulder.

Right front: work sts #1–4 of the pattern repeat from Chart 1, including increases: (inc 1), 1 st in pattern, pick up and knit 1 additional st for the neckline from the I-cord of the collar [= 4 sts].

WS: (reading Row 2 of Chart 1 from left to right)

Right front: work sts #9–12 of the pattern repeat, including increase, work the 1st st of the pattern repeat once: 3 sts in pattern, (inc 1) [= 5 sts].

P3 in Blue for the shoulder.

Back: including increases, work st #1 of the pattern repeat, work the pattern repeat 3 times widthwise, work st #12 of the pattern repeat: (inc 1), 34 sts in pattern, (inc 1) [= 38 sts].

P3 in Blue for the shoulder.

Left front: including increases, work st #1 of the pattern repeat, work sts #12–9 of the pattern repeat: (inc 1), 3 sts in pattern [= 5 sts].

Rep shoulder increases 13 (23) times more and rep additional increases for the front neckline in every RS row 8 times more, continuing the colorwork pattern according to Chart 1. After the shoulder increases, the colorwork pattern will end on st #3 (12) of the pattern repeat, and after the additional increases for the neckline, it will end on a full pattern repeat plus 1 stitch, which is worked in Blue [front = 27 (37) sts, back = 64 (84) sts].

Now, working in White, continue on the I-cord of the collar.

At the end of the last RS row (right half of the collar), take up the previously held 3 I-cord sts of the collar, place them on the left needle, and knit them.

Turn work, *slip sts #1+2 purlwise, work pfb in the 3rd stitch, tightening the working yarn to avoid an unsightly hole. Turn work, sl1, k3*, turn work, and rep the steps from * to * 9 times more = 10 sts picked up + 3 I-cord sts.

After all 10 sts have been picked up, work the 3 I-cord sts again as previously described, and also work 9 sts in White, 1 st in Blue in stockinette stitch.

Now, work to the end of the WS row, place the 3 unworked I-cord sts of the left half of the collar onto the left needle and work them, turn work.

As described before, pick up and knit 10 additional sts for the left front, this time, however, knit the sts = 40 (50) sts for the front.

BUTTON BAND/BUTTONHOLE BAND, BEGINNING OF SLEEVES

Button band/buttonhole band and sleeve are worked according to Chart 2.

Left front: 3 sts I-cord in White, 1 full pattern repeat according to Chart 2, 2 sts in Blue, continue 26 (36) sts in pattern according to Chart 1 in the same manner.

Left sleeve: The 3 shoulder sts transition into the sleeve sts, including increases: 1 st in Blue, work sts #4–6 of the pattern repeat, (inc 1) in pattern (Blue), (inc 1) [= 5 sts].

Back: including increases, continue the pattern from Chart 1 over 86 sts in the same manner.

Right sleeve: The 3 shoulder sts transition into the sleeve sts, including increases: 1 st in Blue, work sts #4–6 of the pattern repeat, (inc 1) in pattern (Blue), 1 st in pattern, (inc 1) [= 5 sts].

Right front: continue the pattern from Chart 1 over 26 (36) sts in the same manner, 2 sts in Blue, work the pattern repeat of Chart 2 once (working sts #2–9 here), 1 st in Blue, 3 I-cord sts in White.

Rep sleeve increases in every row 11 times more, then in every other row (always in a RS row) 13 times more, continue the colorwork pattern according to Chart 2 in the same manner, and to the right of (before) it and to the left of (after) it, keep working 1 st in Blue.

Then, cast on additional underarm sts on the front and back as follows:

Work all sts of the left front in established pattern, inc 1 (see explanations in chapter Basics on pages 17–18) in pattern, 1 st in Blue, inc 1 in pattern, work over the left sleeve sts in pattern to the last blue stitch, inc 1 in pattern, 1 st in Blue, inc 1 in pattern, work all sts of the back in established pattern, inc 1 in pattern, 1 st in Blue, inc 1 in pattern, work over the right sleeve sts in pattern to the last blue stitch, inc 1 in pattern, 1 st in Blue, inc 1 in pattern, work all sts of the right front in established pattern.

Rep increases in every other row on the front and back (always in a RS row) 5 times more; on the sleeves, for Size S–M 3 times more, for Size L–XL 5 times more (resulting in 46 (56) sts for each front, 61 (65) sts for each sleeve, and 76 (86) sts for the back).

DIVIDING THE SLEEVES FROM THE BODY

Work the 46 (56) sts of the right front in established pattern, transfer 61 (65) sleeve sts to a piece of waste yarn or spare cord for holding, with both strands of working yarn held together, cast on 8 (12) new

underarm sts, work the 76 (84) sts of the back in established pattern, transfer the next 61 (65) sleeve sts to a piece of waste yarn or spare cord for holding, with both strands of working yarn held together, cast on 8 (12) new underarm sts, work the 46 (56) sts of the left front in established pattern [= 184 (220) sts].

Work another 11 in/28 cm in pattern.

Work 2 rows in the following manner: 3 sts I-cord, 9 sts button band/buttonhole band, 158 (194) sts in Blue, 9 sts button band/buttonhole band, 3 sts I-cord, within the 158 (194) sts, increase 3 sts evenly spaced [= 187 (223) sts].

Now, work 6 rows as follows:

3 sts I-cord, work the pattern repeat of Chart 2 (9 sts in width) 20 (24) times widthwise, 1 st in Blue, 3 sts I-cord, break the working yarn in Blue.

Then, using White and applied I-cord bind-off method, bind off all sts to the end of the back, transfer the 3 I-cord sts to a safety pin or piece of waste yarn for holding.

Now, bind off the I-cord sts of the right front from the wrong side in purl. Neatly join the beginning and end of the I-cord by grafting the I-cord sts, now next to each other, in Kitchener stitch.

SLEEVES

Take up the 61 (65) sleeve sts again, place them onto a circular knitting needle, and pick up and knit 9 (14) underarm sts from the armhole edge at the side of the body (picking up at a rate of more than 1 st from each st where necessary to reach the stitch count), picking up an additional st each at the corners, and placing a marker to indicate the BOR after half of the picked-up sts [= 72 (81) sts].

Continue to work the stranded colorwork pattern according to Chart 2, incorporating the 1st and the last st in Blue into the pattern and likewise incorporating the underarm sts into the pattern.

Work an additional 14.2 in/36 cm in pattern, ending with a Row 6 of the chart.

Work 2 rounds in Blue in stockinette stitch, during the last round decreasing 14 sts evenly spaced [= 58 (67) sts].

Work 20 rounds in White in garter stitch, then bind off all sts knitwise.

FINISHING

Carefully weave in all ends. Wash the cardigan according to the manufacturer's washing instructions on the ball band of the yarn, and let it dry spread out flat on an even horizontal surface.

CHART 1

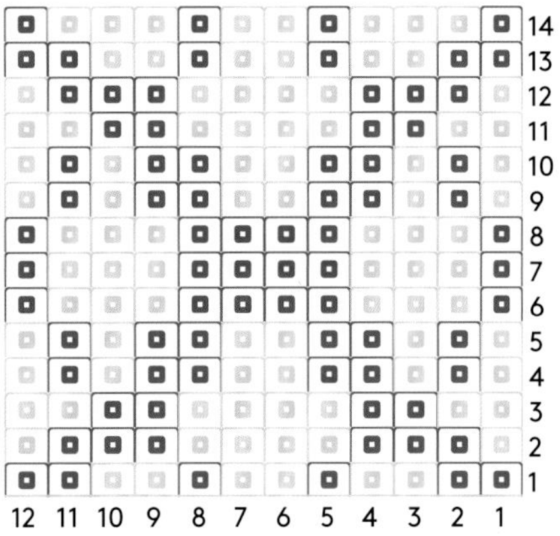

CHART 2

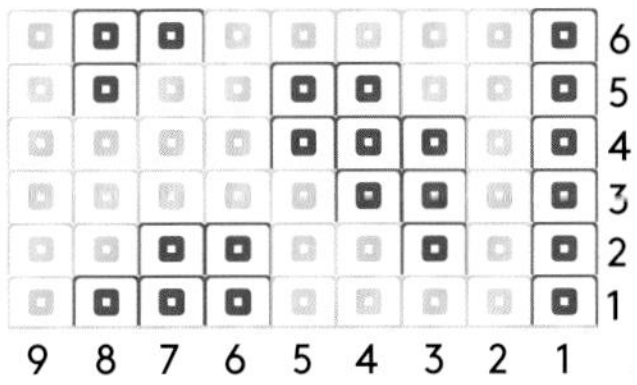

ABOUT THE AUTHOR

Even as a small child, Andrea Brauneis had a passion for wool and crafts. Knitting quickly emerged as a favorite hobby, and later she was able to turn it into a full-time career. Professional design training with an emphasis on practical aspects and many workshops—primarily in Scandinavia and Scotland—enabled her to constantly expand her knowledge. She now works as a freelance designer and is the author of several knitting books, including *Knitting Wraps in the Round*. She lives with her family in Munich, Germany, and can be found on Instagram @andrea.brauneis.

THANK YOU

YARN SUPPORT

Lang Yarns

Isager

Paul Pascuali

Rosy Green Wool

Holst Garn

Rauma Garn

Jamieson & Smith—Real Shetland Wool

Jim Knopf (buttons)

Thank you very much for your generous contribution of beautiful yarns and pretty buttons, with which it was a special pleasure to knit and work!

SAMPLE AND TEST KNITTERS

Heartfelt thanks for your amazing cooperation, your time, and your skills—you have knitted beautiful projects and done a marvelous job:

Lila Winter, Regina Schürmann, Christine Mai, Lilly Mauer, Nora König, Nina Bühler, and Luise Mayer.